Quick Guide

Floors

D0731373

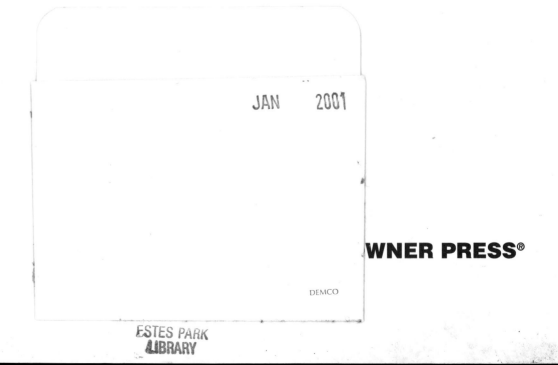

JAN   2001

DEMCO

WNER PRESS®

COPYRIGHT © 1998, 1992
CREATIVE HOMEOWNER PRESS®
A Division of Federal Marketing Corp.
Upper Saddle River, NJ

Quick Guide is a registered trademark of Creative Homeowner Press®

Manufactured in the United States of America

Creative Director: Warren Ramezzana
Editor: Arnie Edelstein
Project Editor: Kimberly Kerrigone
Graphic Designer: Annie Jeon
Illustrators: James Randolph, Norman Nuding
Production Assistant: Mindy Circelli
Technical Reviewer: Jim Barrett

Cover Design: Warren Ramezzana
Cover Illustrations: Moffit Cecil

Electronic Prepress and Printing:
Command Web Offset, Inc.

Current Printing (last digit)
10 9 8 7 6 5

Quick Guide: Floors
LC: 92-81621
ISBN: 1-880029-06-5 (paper)

CREATIVE HOMEOWNER PRESS®
A Division of Federal Marketing Corp.
24 Park Way
Upper Saddle River, NJ 07458

C O N T E N T S

Though all the designs and methods in this book have been tested for safety, it is not possible to overstate the importance of using the safest construction methods possible. What follows are reminders; some do's and don'ts of basic carpentry. They are not substitutes for your own common sense.

- *Always* use caution, care, and good judgment when following the procedures described in this book.

- *Always* be sure that the electrical setup is safe; be sure that no circuit is overloaded and that all power tools and electrical outlets are properly grounded. Do not use power tools in wet locations.

- *Always* read container labels on paints, solvents, and other products; provide ventilation, and observe all other warnings.

- *Always* read the manufacturer's instructions for using a tool, especially the warnings.

- *Always* use hold-downs and push sticks whenever possible when working on a table saw. Avoid working short pieces if you can.

- *Always* remove the key from any drill chuck (portable or press) before starting the drill.

- *Always* pay deliberate attention to how a tool works so that you can avoid being injured.

- *Always* know the limitations of your tools. Do not try to force them to do what they were not designed to do.

- *Always* make sure that any adjustment is locked before proceeding. For example, always check the rip fence on a table saw or the bevel adjustment on a portable saw before starting to work.

- *Always* clamp small pieces firmly to a bench or other work surface when using a power tool on them.

- *Always* wear the appropriate rubber or work gloves when handling chemicals, moving or stacking lumber, or doing heavy construction.

- *Always* wear a disposable face mask when you create dust by sawing or sanding. Use a special filtering respirator when working with toxic substances and solvents.

- *Always* wear eye protection, especially when using power tools or striking metal on metal or concrete; a chip can fly off, for example, when chiseling concrete.

- *Always* be aware that there is seldom enough time for your body's reflexes to save you from injury from a power tool in a dangerous situation; everything happens too fast. Be *alert!*

- *Always* keep your hands away from the business ends of blades, cutters, and bits.

- *Always* hold a circular saw firmly, usually with both hands so that you know where they are.

- *Always* use a drill with an auxiliary handle to control the torque when large-size bits are used.

- *Always* check your local building codes when planning new construction. The codes are intended to protect public safety and should be observed to the letter.

- *Never* work with power tools when you are tired or under the influence of alcohol or drugs.

- *Never* cut tiny pieces of wood or pipe using a power saw. Cut small pieces off larger pieces.

- *Never* change a saw blade or a drill or router bit unless the power cord is unplugged. Do not depend on the switch being off; you might accidentally hit it.

- *Never* work in insufficient lighting.

- *Never* work while wearing loose clothing, hanging hair, open cuffs, or jewelry.

- *Never* work with dull tools. Have them sharpened, or learn how to sharpen them yourself.

- *Never* use a power tool on a workpiece—large or small—that is not firmly supported.

- *Never* saw a workpiece that spans a large distance between horses without close support on each side of the cut; the piece can bend, closing on and jamming the blade, causing saw kickback.

- *Never* support a workpiece from underneath with your leg or other part of your body when sawing.

- *Never* carry sharp or pointed tools, such as utility knives, awls, or chisels, in your pocket. If you want to carry such tools, use a special-purpose tool belt with leather pockets and holders.

ANATOMY OF FLOORS

There are three basic types of floors covered in this chapter: concrete floors, wood floors over concrete, and floors on subflooring laid over joists. The chapter opens with a description of the tools that you will need in order to accomplish the projects in this book. Then it details the three types of floors and how each is built.

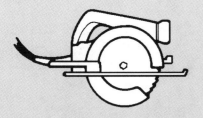

Circular Saw. This portable power saw cuts more quickly than a hand crosscut or rip saw. The base plate (which rides on the material being cut) can be adjusted to cut angles. Different materials, from paneling to brick, can be cut with appropriate blades.

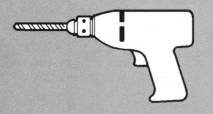

Electric Drill. With various accessories, the power drill can be used to sand, to cut circular holes, to drive screws, and to perform several other tasks. Drills are available in different sizes—given as the size of the largest bit they can accept—and with various power features, such as variable speed.

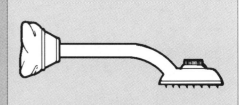

Knee-Kicker. Essential for laying a wall-to-wall carpet tightly, the knee-kicker grips the carpet with teeth so you can stretch it toward the walls with a push from your knee on the padded end. A larger device, called a power stretcher, performs the same function without the knee power.

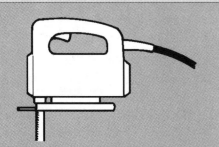

Saber Saw. Extremely useful for cutting irregular shapes and making interior cuts, the narrow blade of the saber saw makes it possible to guide it through fairly tight curves and to start cuts through a hole drilled inside an area to be cut out. There are many blades available for cutting different materials.

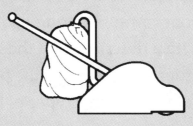

Floor Sander. Unless you restore floors professionally, you will not need to invest in a floor sander. They can be rented from most home centers which also supply the sandpaper replacements. There are belt sanders and circular sanders for floors; the circular sander can be used for buffing as well.

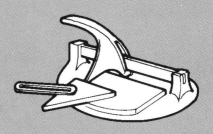

Tile Cutter. The cutter holds a piece of tile in place so that it can be scored by a cutting wheel attached to the handle of the cutter. When the tile is scored, it is broken neatly along that line by a pull on the handle. Unless you do a lot of tiling, it is more economical to rent the cutter.

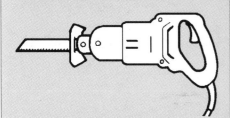

Reciprocating Saw. Like a heavy-duty saber saw, this power saw is handy for cutting out sections of walls or floors, or cutting through a roof for a skylight. These saws are available in one, two, or variable speed models with a variety of blades for different jobs. This is not a tool to buy to do just one project.

Floor Nailer. This device makes the tedious, tricky job of nailing hardwood flooring proceed more quickly and accurately. The floor nailer is loaded with a clip of nails, which it drives by spring action when hit smartly on the top knob with a mallet. You can rent one for laying a wood strip floor.

Plane. There are many kinds of planes for different work: The two kinds you may need for these projects are the small block plane, a one-handed tool for rounding corners and removing small amounts of wood; and the jack plane, a two-handed model for larger general planing jobs.

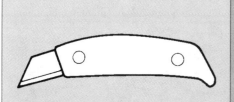

Utility Knife. Best for cutting building paper, wallboard, and many other relatively soft materials, the utility knife has razor-sharp replaceable blades.

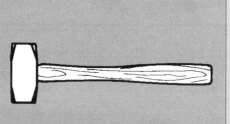

Sledgehammer. Available in various weights up to 20 pounds, the sledgehammer is used for demolition and for driving heavy objects, such as posts, into place.

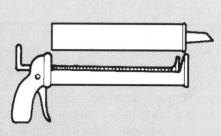

Caulking Gun. A standard-size holder for tubes of caulking or adhesive, this spring-loaded device dispenses an even bead that is easy to apply and manipulate.

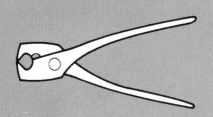

Tile Nippers. A tile cutter will cut only straight lines, so tile nippers are used for irregular cuts which are made by nipping away small pieces of tile.

Notched Trowel. Used to spread adhesive for setting ceramic and other tile. Different adhesives call for different sized notches so check your product.

Star Drill. The star drill, for making holes in masonry, takes a lot of effort. It is driven with a 5-pound hammer and rotated slightly after each blow.

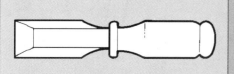

Chisels. Available in a great variety of types and sizes, chisels are used for gouging and trimming. Your hardware dealer can match a chisel to your specific needs.

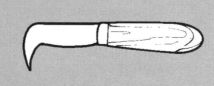

Linoleum Knife. The hooked blade, stronger than that on a utility knife, makes it easier and more accurate to cut tough resilient sheet flooring than with any other blade.

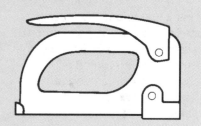

Staple Gun. A heavy-duty staple gun or staple hammer will make many projects go quickly. It is essential for installing ceiling tile and for stapling insulation between boards.

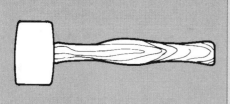

Mallet. This heavy hammer has a soft head of rubber, plastic, or leather. It is used when weight is required and a metal head would do damage (e.g., when operating a floor nailer).

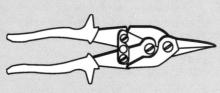

Shears. Heavy shears are necessary to cut various metal home improvement materials like aluminum studs and tracks, wire lath, and corner bead.

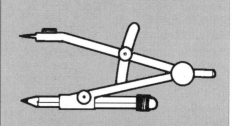

Compass. You can use a compass or scriber for tracing an irregular edge onto a piece of board or sheet of paneling that must be cut to fit the irregularity exactly.

Concrete Floors

Creating a concrete floor can turn an unfinished basement or garage into more usable space and at the same time reduce dampness. Before beginning any work, however, research the local building codes to see that the height of the ceiling is a legal distance from the floor. Also, you may be required to have an on-the-scene inspection of the grading job before pouring the concrete.

Pouring goes rather quickly, but preliminary preparations should be planned and executed with care. You will have to grade the subsurface and add a layer of gravel, plastic liners and steel reinforcements. A slanted drainage grade must be built to lead water to one corner of the room where, if need be, you may install a sump pump. In addition, you should dredge channels around the perimeter, and diagonally across the room, for installing drain pipes made of plastic tubing perforated to dissipate water through the gravel.

The truck that brings the ready-mix concrete may have to drive up onto your property to within 10 feet of the basement window for the chute to reach. Prepare the ground around the area with 2x10 planks and poly-ethylene sheeting to catch any spills.

Pour the concrete and spread it rapidly. For best results, fill one section of the floor at a time before going on to the next. Then use a screed and a darby to remove excess concrete and smooth down aggregate that may rise to the surface. Allow "bleed water" to bubble up and disappear before you trowel the surface to a smooth finish and cut control joints.

When all is completed, the concrete slab must cure; the chemicals must interact with water to render the floor strong and durable. You can purchase a curing compound from a building supplier or keep the floor damp for a week or longer.

Preparing the Grade

1 Leveling the Old Floor.
Remove the soil of the old dirt floor so that the surface is 8 inches below the level where the surface of the concrete floor will be. The floor should slope 1 inch every 8 feet to the lowest corner where the sump pump will be located. Snap chalk lines on the walls at the finish floor height, and tie string across the room to nails located every 4 feet along the chalk line to check slope.

2 Digging Out for a Sump. Dig a hole 2½ feet deep and 2 feet wide in the lowest corner of the room for the sump pump. If you are not using a sump pump, fill the hole with clean gravel. Remove the strings. Then dig a trench 4 inches deep and 6 inches wide about 5 inches from the walls around the room, and a similar trench diagonally across the room. Pour a 2-inch layer of gravel into the trenches, and on it lay lengths of drain tile or 3-inch perforated plastic pipe with holes facing down to form a conduit around and across the room, so that the ends drain into the hole or are attached to the sump pump.

Preparing to Pour

3 Putting in the Forms. Make key-jointed form boards by nailing 1x2s (with a 1/4-inch bevel on the edges) to the middle of as many 2x4s as you will need to span the length of the room (and to span half its width if the floor is to be poured in smaller sections). Then drill three 3/4-inch holes in each board, one in the center, and two a foot from both ends. Nail three stakes (16-inch 1x2s) on the back of each form board so that the top of each stake is flush with the upper edge of the form board. Drive the stakes into the dirt floor so that it divides the basement in two. The key-joint molds should face the side of the room you intend to pour first. Make sure the form is at the finished floor elevation and, using a level, check the grade of the form.

1 Dig out the old floor 8 in. below the level wanted for the new floor; use string guides to keep depth even.

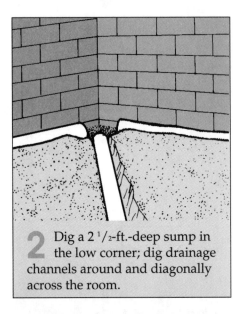

2 Dig a 2½-ft.-deep sump in the low corner; dig drainage channels around and diagonally across the room.

3 Have a helper hold the key-jointed form. Drive the stakes down to the level indicated by the string.

4 **Laying Reinforcing Mesh.** Pour a 4-inch layer of gravel over the graded dirt floor. Insert 1-foot steel reinforcing bars (rebar) into gravel every 2 or 3 feet. Spread polyethylene sheets over the gravel overlapping about 18 inches and extending up the walls to the chalk lines. Lay reinforcing wire mesh.

5 **Shoring Up the Form.** Insert 18-inch steel rebar 1/2 inch in diameter through the holes in the form boards so that half the rebar is on each side. Use wooden wedges in the back of the form to hold the rebar in place. Pack gravel up tightly behind the form boards. Lastly, rub grease on the forms so the concrete will not bond to them.

Spreading the Concrete

6 **Initial Spreading.** Use a hoe and a shovel to spread the concrete. When a section is filled, use a rake to pull the reinforcing wire halfway up through the wet concrete.

7 **Leveling the Slab.** Using a screed, level a section of the wet slab up to the rebar and pound them beneath the concrete surface with a sledgehammer. Then work the area level to the top of the form boards and nails in the wall.

8 **Smoothing the Surface.** Smooth the leveled surface with a darby. "Bleed water" will appear on the top of the slab, making it shiny. When completely dry, the surface will be dull.

9 **Finishing.** When the concrete can withstand the toss of a 1-inch stone so that it bounces, leaving only a slight indentation, cut 1-inch-deep control joints every 10 feet. Then smooth the surface between the joints with a wooden float and a steel trowel, moving backward. If the concrete is too hard, dampen it a bit. In 5 to 6 hours wet the surface again and cover with polyethylene sheets for 24 hours. Then remove the forms and gravel packing, and pour the companion slab.

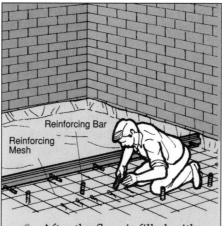

4 After the floor is filled with 4 in. of gravel covered with a plastic sheet, lay mesh and attach pieces.

5 After placing steel rebar into the form, bank up gravel behind it to hold it in place and to hold back the concrete.

6 Spread concrete from where it is dumped, then roughly level the surface with a rake.

7 Make a screed from pieces of 2x4 and level the surface to the top of the form.

8 Use a large rented float called a darby to smooth the surface; then wait until the surface becomes dull.

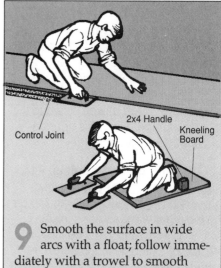

9 Smooth the surface in wide arcs with a float; follow immediately with a trowel to smooth away the marks left by the float.

Installing Wood Floors Over Concrete

If you plan to cover concrete with a wood floor, you have two options: Build directly onto it or build a new subfloor over it. If the concrete is level, lay sleepers down and nail the new floor onto them as you would on floor beams. If the concrete is too uneven, it is best to build another subfloor suspended over the concrete base. If you are building directly onto a cement floor that is not level, you will have to resurface the concrete to make it level. A new floor cannot be built onto one that is uneven.

In deciding which option to follow, take the following factors into consideration. Some concrete floors sweat, and unless they are properly lined with damp-proof polyethylene sheets, moisture will rot the wood. If you build directly onto the concrete by means of sleepers, you should install sheets of polyethylene under the sleepers, thus creating a thin film that is moisture resistant. If heating the room will be problematic, do not build directly onto the concrete. Instead, raise the floor by adding a new subfloor and install insulation beneath the subfloor to prevent heat loss.

Suspending a Subfloor over Concrete

1 Finding the Level Line. Locate a level line on each stud by use of a water level. Measure the distance from the level line to where you want the subfloor by using a template of wood sawed down to the exact distance. Mark this spot on each stud with a chalk line.

2 Attaching Header Joists. Attach 2x6 boards for header joists along the two longest walls and 2x6s on the other walls as band joists. Make sure that the joists butt in the middle of a stud. Use three 10d common nails at each end of the joist to anchor it to a stud. The edge of the joists should touch the chalk line and be level, regardless of any variation in distance from the existing floor.

3 Installing a Girder Beam. If the room is wider than 12 feet, you will need to install a girder for added strength. You can construct a girder beam by spiking two 2x8 boards together in four sections. In a 20-foot room, lay a 16-foot board so that it butts a 4-foot board and spike a second 16-foot board to both. Add another 4-foot board to the top of the two bottom boards and you will have a girder beam of double thickness. Turn the beam on its side, crown side up, and nail it to the band joists (using a framing hanger) so that its top will be flush with the top of the joists. Shore up the center of the girder beam with blocks of wood. The girder and joists should be level. Check with a carpenter's level as you work.

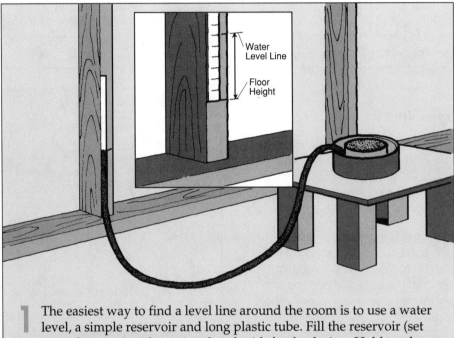

1 The easiest way to find a level line around the room is to use a water level, a simple reservoir and long plastic tube. Fill the reservoir (set at correct elevation) with water colored with food coloring. Hold up the end of the tube, and mark at the waterline on the walls.

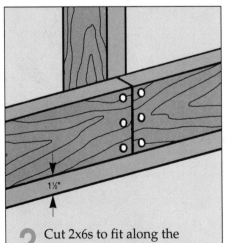

2 Cut 2x6s to fit along the longest walls; butt pieces if necessary. Nail along the walls below the chalk line.

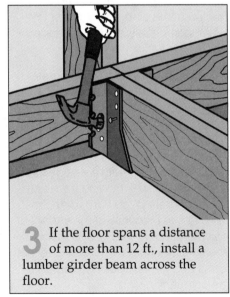

3 If the floor spans a distance of more than 12 ft., install a lumber girder beam across the floor.

4 **Installing Floor Joists.** The joists are nailed to the header joists and girder beam using framing hangers. Measure 15¼ inches from the end of the header joist for the first floor joist and every 16 inches thereafter to the opposite wall. Attach floor joists every 16 inches. As you proceed, unroll a sheet of polyethylene to serve as a moisture barrier. Staple the edges to the perimeter joists.

5 **Attaching Legs.** To each floor joist nail three legs of scrap lumber, one at each end and one in the middle, so that one end of the leg touches the floor and the other is lower than the top edge of the joist. When you have finished nailing all the floor joists and their legs, staple insulation over the joists, fiberglass down.

6 **Installing the Floor.** If your floor joists are exactly 16 inches apart, 4x8 plywood can be laid conventionally, the seams of the subfloor meeting in the center of a beam. Use 6d coated nails every 6 inches along the edges and every 10 inches in the field. Use a half sheet to begin every other row so that the seams are staggered.

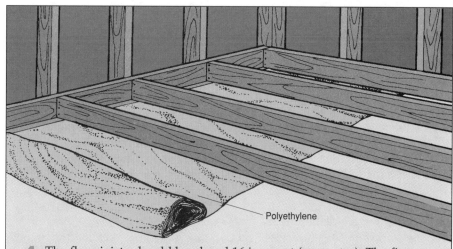

Polyethylene

4 The floor joists should be placed 16 in. apart (on center). The first and last joists are the band joists.

5 Nail scrap lumber legs onto the floor a little below the tops of the joists and just touching the floor. Insulate the joists.

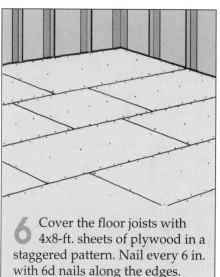

6 Cover the floor joists with 4x8-ft. sheets of plywood in a staggered pattern. Nail every 6 in. with 6d nails along the edges.

Laying Wood Directly on a Concrete Floor

If your concrete floor is dry and level and insulation is not a concern, you can dispense with subflooring and install a floor directly on pressure-treated sleepers that have been set in adhesive on the concrete. After concrete is sealed, wood strip flooring may be nailed directly onto the sleepers. Apply a coat of sealer to the concrete floor and allow it to dry. Then apply an exterior grade adhesive (or an asphalt mastic made for bonding wood to concrete) in ribbons

about 1/8 inch thick and 4 inches wide along the border of the room. Lay the first treated 2x4 sleepers along the border, with the 3½-inch side in the adhesive. Next, lay rows of sleepers 18 to 48 inches long, allowing about 10 inches between rows. The first piece should touch the border on one wall. Continue laying each sleeper alongside the previous one, letting their ends overlap 4 to 6 inches. Secure each sleeper with at least two concrete nails.

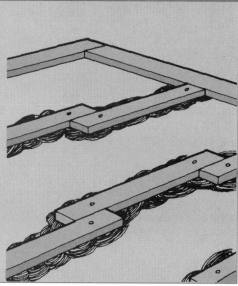

Joist Floors

For a structure with a basement or crawl space, a concrete footing is poured below the frost line, then a concrete or concrete block foundation wall is erected on it, with anchor bolts embedded in the top about every 4 feet, protruding at least 2¼ inches. (These and all other dimensions given in this chapter should be checked against local design considerations and building codes.) In concrete-slab construction, the slab itself serves as the platform on which the walls are built; anchor bolts are embedded around the perimeter.

Floor joists normally run across the narrow width of the foundation. If the structure is no more than 14 or 15 feet wide (check codes), the joists may span the full width. For greater spans, a girder or beam is placed along the centerline to support the joists. The girder may be wood (usually three pieces of 2x8, 2x10, or 2x12 nailed together) or a steel I-beam recessed into the foundation wall. A wood beam is set with its top 1½ inches above the foundation, level with the sill plates. Often, an I-beam is set flush with the top of the foundation, and then a length of 2x4 or 2x6 is fastened on top of it so that it is level with the sill. The girder is supported at 8- to 10-foot intervals by posts resting on concrete footings. The posts are either 4x6 or larger timbers or steel lally columns.

The sill or sill plate consists of lengths of lumber (usually 2x6s) laid flat on the foundation wall to provide a bearing surface for the floor joists. The sill is drilled to fit over the anchor bolts and laid in a bed of mortar or fiberglass sealer. Flat washers fit over the bolts, and nuts are tightened to hold the sill securely. (Where there is danger of termite invasion, a metal shield is placed between the foundation and the sill.)

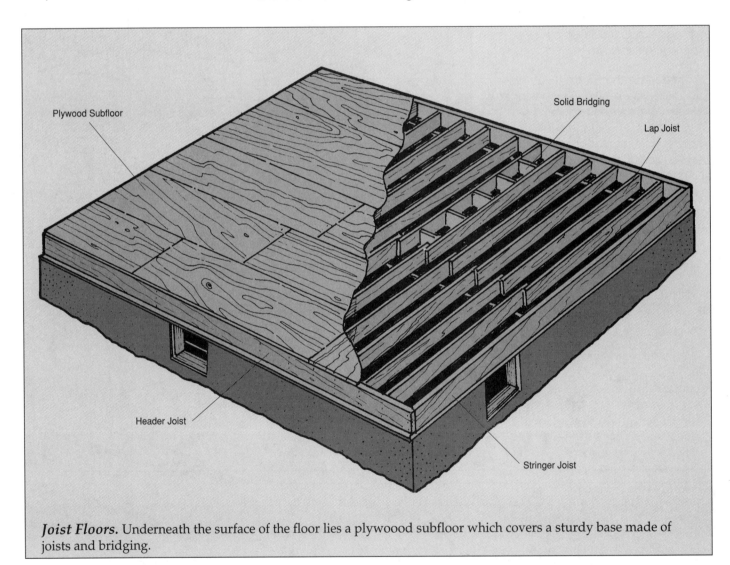

Plywood Subfloor

Solid Bridging

Lap Joist

Header Joist

Stringer Joist

Joist Floors. Underneath the surface of the floor lies a plywoood subfloor which covers a sturdy base made of joists and bridging.

Joist System. Floor joists are the main supporting members of the floor. They rest on the sill at the outside and on the girder at the inner end. Depending on the span and the floor load, joists are most commonly 2x8s, 2x10s, or sometimes 2x12s that are set on edge. They are usually spaced 16 inches on center, which means from the center of each board. Joists overlap at the girder, so this must be taken into account when laying out the positions on the sill plates.

Where partitions on the floor above will run parallel to the joists, double joists are usually provided to carry the weight. If heating ducts or plumbing pipes will be run through the partition, the joists are usually spaced so that they will be on each side of the partition, rather than directly beneath it (unless this interferes with the 16-inch on-center spacing pattern). Openings for basement stairways, crawl space access, and chimneys require double joists and headers all around, but again, these should not alter the regular joist spacing. Header joists and band joists enclose the perimeter of the floor framing.

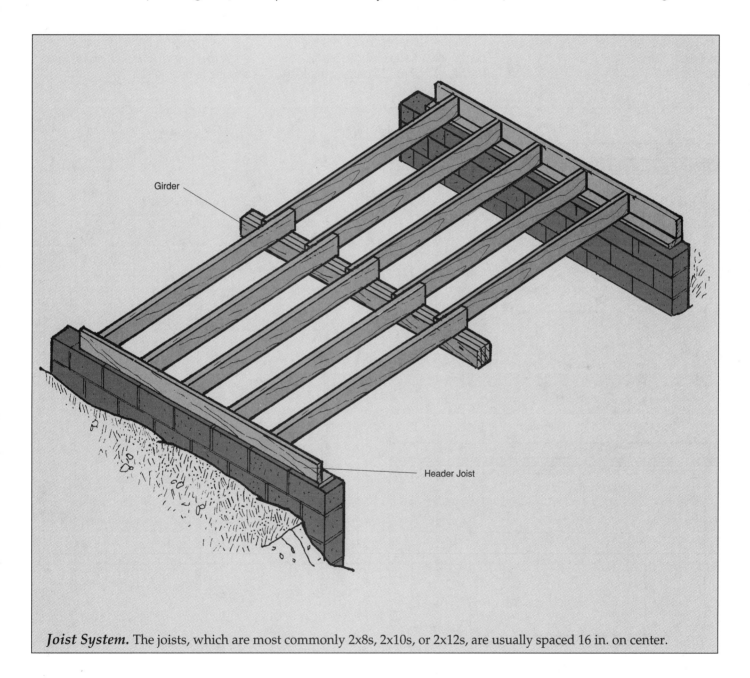

Girder

Header Joist

Joist System. The joists, which are most commonly 2x8s, 2x10s, or 2x12s, are usually spaced 16 in. on center.

Cross Bridging. Cross bridging consists of diagonal pieces of wood (1x3s, 1x4s, or 2x2s) arranged in an X pattern between adjacent joists, midway between sill and girder. Recent research has questioned the benefits of cross bridging, indicating that it shows no significant ability to transfer loads after the subfloor and finish floor are installed. Still, cross bridging is required by many building codes. When used, it is nailed at the top first. The lower ends are left loose until the subfloor is laid; then they are nailed.

Solid Bridging. Usually a piece of lumber the same size as the joist is used between joists to provide a more rigid base for partitions above joist spaces. Solid bridging also is used where irregular spacing may make it difficult to install cross bridging.

Subflooring. This surface is nailed (sometimes glued) over the joists. Plywood is the material of choice for subflooring; it goes down quickly and covers large areas in minimal time. C-D interior plywood (3/4 inch) is commonly used for subflooring. Panels of this grade carry a marking

that shows the allowable spacing of joists for various thicknesses of plywood. A marking of 32/16 means that spacing can be 32 inches if the panel is to be used for roof sheathing; 16 inches, for subflooring. The plywood should be laid with the better (C) face up. Grain direction of outer plies should be at right angles to the joists. Panels should be staggered so that end joints in adjacent panels fall over different joists (the ends must always be centered on a joist). Allow 1/8-inch spacing between panels at edge joints and 1/16-inch spacing at end joints over joists.

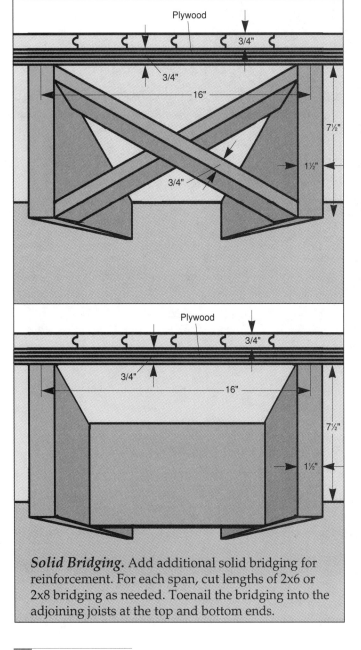

Solid Bridging. Add additional solid bridging for reinforcement. For each span, cut lengths of 2x6 or 2x8 bridging as needed. Toenail the bridging into the adjoining joists at the top and bottom ends.

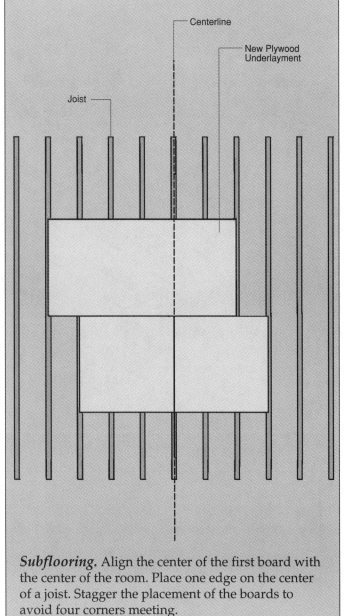

Subflooring. Align the center of the first board with the center of the room. Place one edge on the center of a joist. Stagger the placement of the boards to avoid four corners meeting.

RESTORING OLD FLOORS

The structure that holds up a house must bear tremendous weight, adjust to seasonal changes of weather, and withstand the constant traffic of those who live in the house. A sagging floor is not rare and can be more often a nuisance than a portent of something disastrous.

Leveling Wood Floors

A 3/4-inch dip in 30 inches or more is a minor problem. Anything larger may be an indication of more serious structural damage such as rotten girders or a termite-ridden post. In older homes where the posts, girders, joists, and bridging are made from the original wood, shifting sometimes occurs. The wood absorbs moisture, especially if the posts are not set on footings, and decay and termites can weaken major supports.

Most sags occur on the first floor where the heaviest furniture and appliances are located and where the major traffic occurs. These can be repaired quite easily from the basement or crawl space. Repairs to second-story floors are more difficult because of cosmetic considerations; the ceiling on the first floor must be removed and replaced, for instance, and a simple jack cannot be left up as a permanent solution. Consult a professional before undertaking any major structural replacement work above the basement level.

For first-floor sags, a telescoping house jack can be installed in the basement to bolster the drooping area. (It functions much like an additional post.) If there is no basement, a smaller, bell-shaped contractor's jack can be rigged up in the crawl space. Use a steel post to replace an old one that is rotten or sinking so that the same problems will not occur later on. When replacing a joist, match the height and length of the old joist and be sure the new one is made of straight, structural-grade lumber free of large knots and cracks, both of which are potential weak spots. Lumber that has been treated with preservatives will tolerate dampness and resist insect infestation better than untreated wood. Replacing joists can be speeded up with a handy tool called a carpenter's nipper, used for clipping protruding nails that cannot be driven up into the finished floor.

Jacking Up a Floor from a Basement

Measure for the deepest point of a sag by laying an 8-foot-long straight-edge across the sagging area of the floor. Mark this point on the basement ceiling by measuring from existing walls. Lock the tubes of a telescoping house jack. Set the bottom plate on a 4x8-inch pad located beneath the sag point. Have a helper hold a 4x6 beam that will span the joists involved in the sag. Screw the jack so that it presses the beam firmly against the joists. Check the jack for plumb, then nail the jack's top and bottom plates to the pad and beam. Raise the jack only 1/16 inch each day until the floor is level—raising it any higher all at once may cause structural damage.

Jacking Up a Floor from a Crawl Space

In the crawl space, build a pyramidal framework out of 6x6s until the pad for the contractor's jack lies close enough to the joists to press a beam against the joists involved in the sag. Raise the jack about 1/16 inch each day, until the sag is corrected.

Strengthening a Weak Joist

1 Fitting the New Joist. Plane one edge of both ends of a new joist, narrowing it by 1/4 inch for about 18 inches. Extract the nails and remove any blocks holding the defective joist to the foundation and the girder.

2 Placing the First Joist. Rest the narrowed ends of the new joist on the girder and sill and position it 1 1/2 inches from the old joist on the sill and against the overlapping joist on the girder. The joist from the other side of the room should be firmly sandwiched between the old and new joists. Drive wooden shims under the planed edges of the new joist so they force it up firmly against the subfloor.

3 Breaking Out the Old Joist. Remove the old joist by cutting it

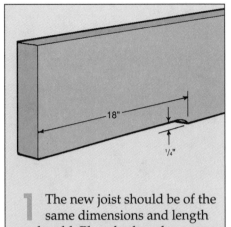

1 The new joist should be of the same dimensions and length as the old. Plane both ends.

2 Set the joist on the far side of the overlapping joist at the girder and shim to force it against the floor.

3 Cut the joist at either end and remove it. Split the ends at the girder and sill, and remove the pieces.

with a saber saw near the girder and foundation sill. Pry it loose from the subfloor with a crowbar and cut the protruding nails flush with the floor. Split the ends of the old joist with a hammer and chisel. Pry the pieces out of the spaces between the subfloor and the girder and sill. Then install a second joist cut in a similar manner to the first. Shim it into place.

4 Installing the Second Joist.
Use 16d nails to nail the new joists to the joist sandwiched between them. Then, about every 3 feet, nail a 2x4 wooden spacer between the joists. Toenail the joists at the girder and foundation sill. Install new bridging where needed. Lastly, go upstairs and drive 8d finishing nails through the floor into the new joist to tie the floor to it and further anchor the joist. If you can't nail through the floor above, install angle brackets on the joist and subfloor using 3/4-inch screws.

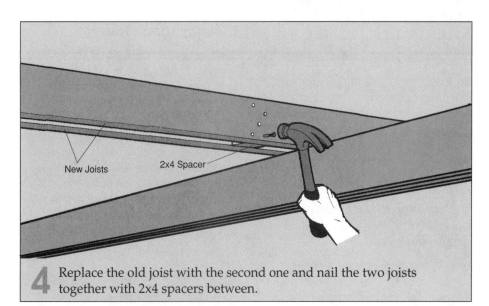

New Joists   2x4 Spacer

4 Replace the old joist with the second one and nail the two joists together with 2x4 spacers between.

Replacing a Post

1. Removing the Old Post. If the girder above the post is spliced, cut away the straps over the splice and replace them with two 3-foot pieces of 1/2-inch plywood. Use 25 to 30 8d nails on each piece. Erect 2 telescoping jacks 3 feet on either side of the old post, and nail the top plates to the girder. Raise the girder 1/16 inch a day until it is completely supported by the jacks and the post is free of any weight. Remove the bolts that attach the post to the girder. With an assistant, tilt the top of the post away from the girder so that it can be lifted off the vertical steel dowel on which it is skewered.

2. Making a New Footing. On the floor, mark a footing the size required by your building code. Use a jackhammer to cut through the concrete floor. Remove all chunks of slab and dig a hole in the subsoil the depth required by code. When all the dirt is removed, dampen the hole and pour the concrete footing while the hole is still wet. The concrete filling should come to a point 4 inches below the floor slab. Release air bubbles by repeatedly thrusting a shovel into the wet concrete. With a straight piece of lumber, level the surface. Cure the concrete for 2 weeks by keeping the surface wet and covered with polyethylene.

3. Setting the New Post. Place the new steel column on the footing and adjust the screw so the top of the column reaches up snugly against the girder. Use the marks from the old post to center the plate. With the holes in the plate as a guide, drill pilot holes into the girder for the 3/8-inch lag screws that will attach the plate to it. Tighten the screws just enough so that you can still move the column at its base. Tap it with a hammer and check with a level on all sides to be sure it is plumb. Tighten the adjusting screw so the post assumes the weight of the girder. Then tighten the lag screws. Release the jacks 1/16 inch a day until they can be taken down. Finish the floor by filling with concrete.

Silencing Squeaking Floors

Squeaky floors are fairly common, there are not many homes that do not have at least one. Although they are aggravating, they do not necessarily indicate anything seriously wrong with the floor or its structure. Usually the squeak is produced by two boards that rub against each other and can be easily silenced either by lubricating the boards that rub or reattaching them.

Many things can cause a floor to squeak: two boards that have warped and rock when they are stepped on; cheaply manufactured floor strips with tongues and grooves that do not fit tightly; a subfloor that has separated from the joists due to settling or due to joists that have dried out, and weak or rotten joists that have separated or have faulty bridging.

Locate the squeak by having someone walk over the noisy area of the floor while you listen and watch from below. Look for springy boards, movement between joists, and bridging that gives when weight is brought to bear. Just to be on the safe side, inspect the area around the squeak for structural damage, which would require more extensive repair such as replacement of girders, posts, or bridging.

Shimming the Subfloor

You can use simple wood shims to silence squeaks that are caused by movement between a joist and loose boards in the subfloor. Locate the squeak and gently tap shims into the space between the joists and the subfloor to prevent movement. Do not drive them too forcefully or they will cause the gap to widen even more by separating the boards from the joist. Wedge them in just firmly enough to fill up the space so that the movement that causes the squeak is eliminated. A dab of adhesive on both sides of the shim will also be helpful.

Cleating the Subfloor

If the squeak is caused by several boards in the subfloor, ones that are laid diagonally, you can eliminate movement by using a 1x4 or 1x6 cleat. Locate the squeaky boards, and place the cleat along the joist that supports the loose boards. Prop it in place with a piece of 2x4 so it will lie snugly against the joist and the subfloor. Then use 8d nails to nail the cleat to the joist. Drive the nails in while the cleat is firmly wedged into the right angle formed by the floor and the joist. When it is solidly attached, remove the 2x4 prop.

Bridging the Joists

Locate the squeak and examine the joists that support the loose boards. If the troublesome area involves boards that span several joists, install steel bridging between them. First, hammer the straight-pronged end into one joist near the top. Then drive the L-shaped flange on the other end into the opposite joist at the bottom, so that the steel

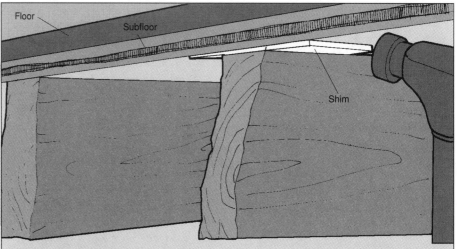

Shimming the Subfloor. If floor joists are not tight against the subfloor in the area that is squeaking, shimming may solve the problem. Wedge shims between the joist and subfloor and tap them into place. Do not pound the shims into place because this will lift the floor and cause additional squeaking.

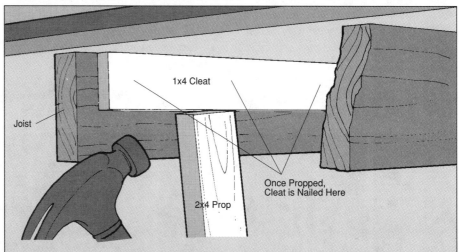

Cleating the Subfloor. Where several boards in a board-type subfloor above a joist are moving, a cleat to hold them is more effective than shimming the boards individually. A piece of 1x4, wedged against the subfloor and nailed to the joist, will keep the subfloor from moving.

bridging creates tension between the two joists. Install the companion bridging in a crisscross fashion and proceed to other joists. The result should be a series of joists more firmly braced and less liable to give beneath the weight of the floor.

Installing Screws from Below

When individual boards are loose or bulging, the resulting squeak can be fixed by pulling the loose boards tightly with screws inserted from below. Use wood screws of a length that will reach to no more than 1/4 inch below the surface of the finish floor. First, drill a pilot hole into the subfloor the size of the screw shank. Put tape on the bit at 3/4 inch so you won't drill into the finish floor. Then drill a pilot hole in the finish floor with a bit slightly smaller than that used for the subfloor. Tape the bit at 1¼ inches so you'll come within 1/4 inch of the finish surface. Insert the screw through a large-diameter washer, and turn it into the hole. As you tighten the screw, it will bite into the finish floorboards and pull them down.

Nailing the Surface

If you cannot gain access to the subfloor, straight nails can be driven through the finish floor to anchor loose boards. Angle 8d finishing nails through the floor so they penetrate a joist if possible. Position the nails in a crisscrossing series. On hardwood floors, drill a pilot hole narrower than the nail, to reduce the chance of splitting the wood. When the nails are in place, set them and fill the hole with wood putty the same color as the floor.

Setting Glazier Points

When a simple squeak caused by two floorboards rubbing together cannot be silenced by lubricants, drive glazier points coated with graphite into the space between the boards. Set the points well below the surface, using a putty knife and a hammer. Space the glazier points 6 inches apart.

Bridging the Joists. Squeaking over a large area may indicate that the joists beneath the floor are shifting slightly and giving inadequate support to the subfloor. Steel bridging, attached between joists, holds the joists from moving side to side and stabilizes the subfloor.

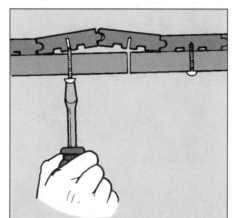

Installing Screws from Below. Drill a pilot hole through the subfloor, then a smaller pilot hole into finish floor. Pull loose boards down with screws.

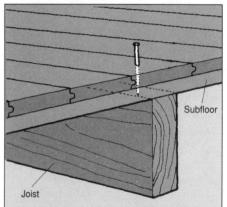

Subfloor

Joist

Nailing the Surface. Nail down from the top with 8d finishing nails when you cannot get access to the floor from below. Try to locate joists and nail into them.

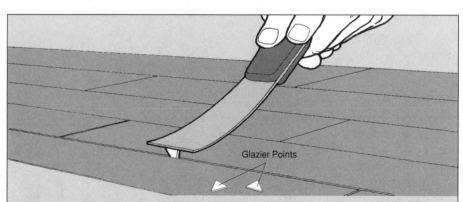

Glazier Points

Setting Glazier Points. Where a squeak is caused by finish floorboards rubbing against one another, you can stop this movement by wedging glazier points between the boards. Lubricate the points with graphite and press them into place with a putty knife. If any stick, tap them with a hammer.

Silencing Squeaky Stairs

The most common cause of squeaky stairs is a loose tread that rubs against other parts of the stairway. If the tread is separated from the riser (the vertical backboard of each step), squeaking will result. Silencing it is a relatively simple matter of determining how the tread and riser are assembled and then closing the gap where the two separate. Techniques for this include: nailing them down, gluing them together, inserting wedges between the gaps, and reinforcing the tread and riser with wooden blocks. Occasionally a tread may be rubbing on the carriage (the diagonal, terraced structure that supports the risers and treads).

To locate the exact spot that causes the squeak, have someone step on each tread and rock back and forth. Observe both the middle of the tread and the ends to determine where the greatest movement occurs. Most squeaks can be eliminated from either above or below. If you can work from underneath the stairs because they rise over a closet or they parallel the basement stairs, fixing them is easier because you do not have to be concerned with the cosmetic effect.

Wedging a Loose Tread

Remove quarter-round molding if you have it. Determine the kind of tread joints by inserting a knife between the tread and riser. Whittle sharp, pointed wedges to 1 or 2 inches long and drive them into the gap between the tread and riser at the points shown. Insert them just enough to silence the squeak. To conceal the wedges, cut off the ends with a utility knife and replace or add quarter-round molding in the joint.

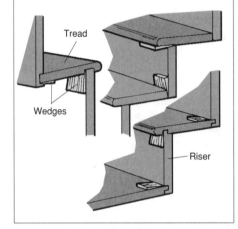

Tread

Wedges

Riser

Nailing & Gluing a Squeaky Tread

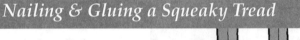

Have a helper stand on the loose tread while you drill 3/32-inch pilot holes at opposing angles through the tread and into the riser at the point of the squeak. If the squeak is near the end of the tread, drill the holes into the carriage. Have a helper apply a line of wood glue between the tread and riser. Then insert two 8d finishing nails and set them while a helper stands on the tread. If nails will not hold the tread, drill an 11/64-inch pilot hole into the tread and a 3/32-inch hole into the riser. Then insert a $2^1/_2$-inch No. 8 wood screw, countersink it and plug the hole with a piece of dowel.

Installing Wood Blocks

Coat two sides of a 2x2 wood block with glue and press it into the joint between the tread and riser. Drive two nails into the riser and one up into the tread. Add as many blocks as are necessary.

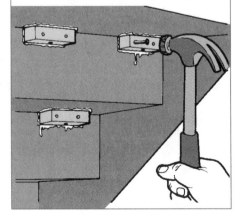

Replacing Loose Wedges in Prefab Stairs

Prefabricated stairs are built with wedges. If they come loose they can create squeaks. Simply split out the old wedge with a chisel and clean out the dried glue. Cut a new wedge to fit, coat the notch with glue, hammer the new wedge firmly into place, but not so hard that it lifts the tread.

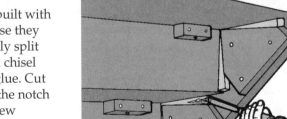

Replacing Damaged Floorboards

The causes of damaged floorboards usually are obvious. Furniture and heavy appliances can mar, crack, and tear wood fibers. Burns and stains also are common causes. If the cause is not immediately obvious, check out the entire floor, not just the damaged area. Also inspect the substructure for sagging girders, settling posts, or moisture and rotting due to plumbing leaks.

When buying replacement boards, take a sample of the old floor to your lumber dealer to make as close a match as possible. Be prepared to discover that nothing matches your floor completely and that you may, therefore, have to refinish the floor when the new boards are in place. A floor made of prefinished boards is not difficult to match although every floor changes with wear and tear over time.

The tools you will need for replacing boards are: a hammer, a 1-inch chisel, a combination square, a pry bar, a portable power saw, 8d finishing nails and wood putty.

There are two methods for replacing floorboards. The easier way requires the removal of a rectangular area that encompasses the damaged boards, leaving a rather noticeable patch; this is not a problem if the floor will be carpeted or the patched area will be under furniture. The second way to go about it is to remove individual boards in a staggered pattern. It is more difficult but the result is less noticeable.

Rectangular Pattern Replacement

1 Making the Cut. With a square and pencil, measure a rectangle encompassing the boards to be removed, marking the lines 1/4 inch from the joints to prevent sawing through nails. Adjust the blade of a portable power saw so that it nearly cuts through the boards. Lower the blade to the wood and work from the center of a line outward. With a hammer and chisel, finish the cut, keeping the beveled side of the chisel facing into the damaged area. Then beginning at the midpoint of a cut side, lift the board out with a pry bar. Use a small block of wood for leverage.

2 Finishing the Cut. Use hammer and chisel to cut away the 1/4 inch remaining behind the saw cuts. Cut carefully and slowly so as not to ruin the edge of the adjacent boards. When the 1/4 inch is removed, set any exposed nail heads in the boards that border the cut area. Next, measure the new boards to be cut; score pencil marks with a saw blade on the waste side of the marks so the kerf will not shorten the board. Lay one end of a scored board tightly into the area where it is to go and double-check the scored mark to make sure it will be the right fit. Then saw it.

3 Nailing New Boards. Lay the new board into place, sliding the grooves over the tongue of the old board. Blind nail the new board with 8d finishing nails driven in at a 45-degree angle through the tongue of the new board. It is not necessary to drill pilot holes first, but it may be helpful to prevent the tongue from splitting. Then lay new boards one at a time in the same manner.

4 Installing the Last Board. First remove the tongue with a saw, and bevel the edge slightly from the bottom to the top. Tap the board into place, using a hammer and a block of wood. Face-nail with 8d finishing nails spaced every 12 inches and driven into pilot holes drilled 1/2 inch from the edges of the face. Set these nails and fill the holes with wood putty. Lastly, sand and seal the new boards and stain them to match the surrounding finish.

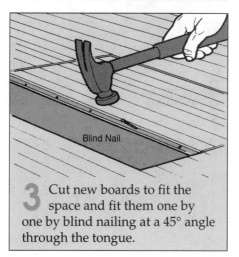

1 Cut around area with a saw set to slightly less than the depth of the finish flooring; finish cut with chisel.

1/4" Space

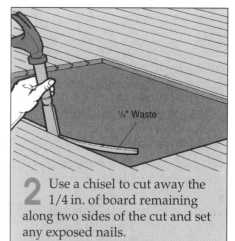

1/4" Waste

2 Use a chisel to cut away the 1/4 in. of board remaining along two sides of the cut and set any exposed nails.

Blind Nail

3 Cut new boards to fit the space and fit them one by one by blind nailing at a 45° angle through the tongue.

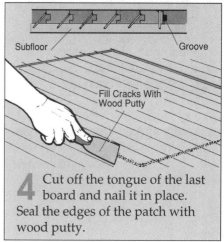

Subfloor · Groove

Fill Cracks With Wood Putty

4 Cut off the tongue of the last board and nail it in place. Seal the edges of the patch with wood putty.

Staggered Pattern Replacement

1 Starting the Cut. With a hammer and chisel make vertical cuts across the boards to be removed with the beveled side of the chisel facing the damaged area. Then angle the chisel toward the vertical cut at 30 degrees and begin to chisel through the board, cutting completely through. The edge of the section not to be removed should be sharp and clean.

2 Finishing the Cut. Split the damaged area by making two rows of incisions with a chisel along the face of the board that has been prepared as shown. Be careful when pounding that you do not damage good boards. Pry up as you move along so that the boards are split through. Then insert a pry bar into the incisions and pry out the middle strip. When it is completely out, pry loose the strip on the groove side of the board, and lastly, the strip on the tongue side. Begin the removal of each strip in the center of the section and work out to the ends. Set any exposed nails you come across.

3 Replacing the Boards. Use a scrap of flooring as a hammering block and tap a cut-to-size replacement board into place sideways so that the groove side goes over the tongue of the old board. Then through the tongue of the new board, drive 8d finishing nails and set them. You may want to drill pilot holes first to avoid splitting the wood.

4 Placing the Last Boards. You cannot slide the last few boards into place. Instead remove the lower lips of their grooves with a chisel and tap the pieces into place from above, securing them with 8d finishing nails driven into pre-drilled holes. Set the nails and fill the holes with matching wood putty.

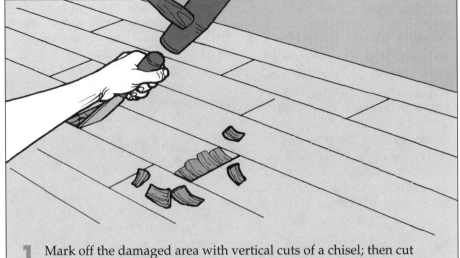

1 Mark off the damaged area with vertical cuts of a chisel; then cut toward these marks at a 30° angle.

2 Break damaged boards with lengthwise cuts and pry out pieces starting with grooved side.

Hammering Block

3 Slip a new board, cut to fit, against the tongue edge of the old floor and tap it into place.

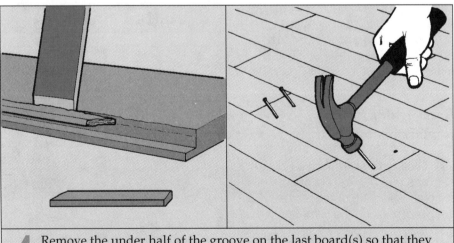

4 Remove the under half of the groove on the last board(s) so that they fit over the tongues of old flooring (left). Fit the boards in place, and attach them with 8d finishing nails driven down into subflooring (right).

Refinishing

Refinishing a floor may seem like a difficult and time-consuming process as you consider it, but the work is largely done by machine. A floor sander can strip an old finish from a floor and create a completely smooth, fresh surface in a matter of two or three hours.

After the floor has been sanded, you may want to stain the flooring, which means you need to fill the pores of the wood before staining and apply a clear sealer. Another alternative is to apply the final finish directly over the freshly sanded wood. The usual choices for a final finish are varnish and urethane varnish.

Sanding the Old Wood Floor

Considerable dust is created when sanding, so wear a dust mask. The masks are sold in paint and hardware stores.

You also should wear goggles or safety glasses, especially if you wear contact lenses. Although the large sander has a vacuum bag and should control much of the dust, the small sander may not have this feature.

1 Cleaning the Floor. Before beginning to sand the floor, check the entire surface for exposed nail heads or raised corners of boards. Either of these can rip a rapidly moving sandpaper belt. Clean the floor of waxy material, which will clog your sandpaper quickly. If the floor has holes, nicks or dents, fill these with appropriately colored wood putty to match the final finish.

2 Removing Baseboards. Although it is not absolutely necessary, you may want to remove the baseboards. If the baseboards need repair and refinishing, you will find the work easier if they are off the wall. Pry the baseboards off carefully; they break easily.

Use a stiff putty knife or a screwdriver with a thin blade. Start at an outside corner and carefully slip the blade between the molding and the wall. Place a thin piece of wood between the prying tool and the wall. This will provide better leverage and protect the wall surface from damage. Use light pressure to pry outward gently. Then move an inch away from the point where you just worked and pry again. Repeat. As you pry, the nails that hold the molding in place will begin to pull free. Continue slowly, in this fashion, so that you do not bend and possibly break the molding.

3 Obtaining Proper Equipment. Floor sanding equipment is usually rented, and you should not have any difficulty in obtaining a unit at your local rental store. You will be supplied with a drum sander, which has rollers that revolve the sandpaper at high speed. You also will need a disc or orbital hand sander for working on the perimeter of the room. All the sandpaper you will require for the job should be part of the rental price—the sandpaper will include coarse, medium, and fine grades.

You also will require a hand scraper for removing the finish in the deepest corners and a vacuum for taking up sanding dust that the sander's vacuum bag misses.

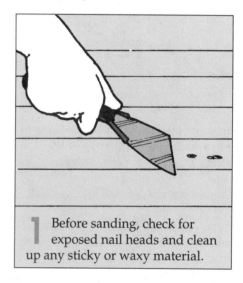

1 Before sanding, check for exposed nail heads and clean up any sticky or waxy material.

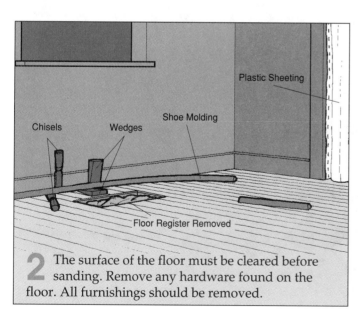

Chisels Wedges Shoe Molding Plastic Sheeting

Floor Register Removed

2 The surface of the floor must be cleared before sanding. Remove any hardware found on the floor. All furnishings should be removed.

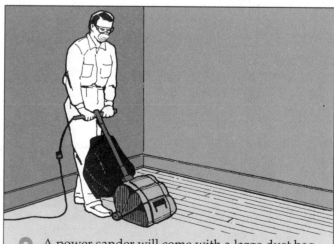

3 A power sander will come with a large dust bag that will control most, but not all, dust. This equipment will make the job much easier.

4 Clearing the Room. Before beginning the sanding process, seal all electrical outlets and switches and all heating ducts and cold air returns. Use duct tape and heavy plastic sheets to cover the openings. Large amounts of airborne dust exposed to an open flame or extreme heat may ignite explosively.

As an additional safety precaution, hang heavy drop sheets on either side of any door leading into the area in which you will be sanding. This will help retain the dust within that area.

Remove everything from the room in which you will work. Take out all furniture, rugs, carpeting, draperies, curtains, window shades. Remove anything that hangs on the walls or is stored in built-in bookcases or cupboards.

Not only will it be easier to work in a completely empty room, but anything left in the room would be exposed to damage from the dust and grit produced during the sanding.

As you work, you will have to remove the dust between sandings and scrupulously clean all surfaces before refinishing. Extraneous objects in the room will merely collect dust that must be removed.
If you leave fabric-covered objects, such as upholstered furniture or drapes in a room, the dust that the sanding produces will get into and between the fibers.

5 Preparing to Sand. Your rental dealer should provide you with full instructions on how to install the sanding belts and how to operate the machine. If he does not, be sure to ask him for full instructions; they will vary from machine to machine. The sander is a big, heavy machine with small metal rollers on which to wheel it when not in use. The sanding belt is one piece and slips over the rollers from one side. The belt is held in place by the pressure of the rollers. In use, the machine is pushed in one direction rather like a lawnmower. There is an on-off switch in the handle.

4 For safety reasons, seal all electrical outlets, switches, heating and air ducts. Hang plastic sheets over doors to keep dust out of adjoining rooms.

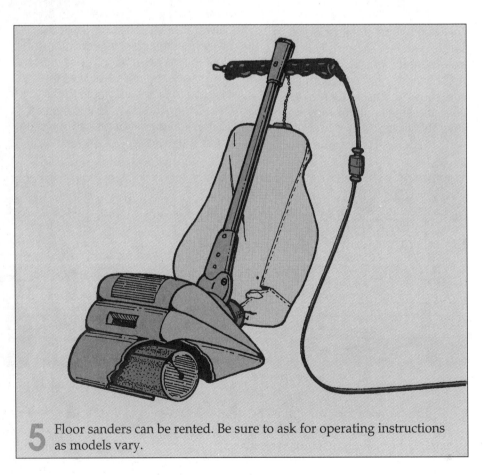

5 Floor sanders can be rented. Be sure to ask for operating instructions as models vary.

6 Rough Sanding. Start in one corner of the room and work diagonally so that you push the sander at an approximately 45-degree angle to the length of the flooring. This will eliminate any irregularities on the edges or joints of the floor planks. Tilt the machine on the roller wheels so the sandpaper belt is NOT in contact with the floor and turn on the machine. Push the machine forward, gradually lowering the machine so that the sandpaper belt makes contact with the floor.

Caution: Some homes may not have sufficient current to run a sander. If a fuse blows or a circuit breaker trips, unplug the machine before replacing the fuse or switching the breaker. Never start the machine with the sandpaper belt touching the floor. Never stop moving the machine when the sandpaper belt is in contact with the floor. Otherwise, you will gouge the floor.

Push the machine to opposite your starting point. As you reach the other side of the room, tilt the machine back and lift the sandpaper belt off the floor.

Move the machine as close to the wall opposite your starting place as you can without touching the wall. Tilt the handle of the machine down to lift the belt off the floor and pull the sander back to your starting point. Resand the same strip until all the finish has been removed. If there is only a single coat of finish on the floor, you may have to go over the strip only once. If there are many layers, you may have to resand two or three times. When the strip is free of finish, roll the machine to an adjacent area and position it so the belt will overlap the first strip by approximately 3 inches.

Repeat this procedure until you have sanded the entire floor and have taken off all the finish. Remember to move the machine slowly but steadily and never stop when the sanding belt is in contact with the floor.

When you have finished with this first rough machine sanding, you still will have a perimeter of unsanded area. Use the hand-held disc sander to remove the finish in this area. Move the hand sander back and forth from left to right. You will have to hold this unit tightly because it will seem to

want to "run away." For this first sanding, use coarse sandpaper, just as you did with the drum sander.

You will be able to do all of the border of the room with the disc sander, except for the absolute corners. To clear the corners, use the hand scraper to scrape the finish off. A small block of wood with a strip of sandpaper wrapped around it also is useful for working in corners. These two tools also will help you remove the floor finish in areas under radiators or other places where the disc sander cannot reach.

It should take approximately one-half hour to rough sand a typical 12x15-foot room.

When the first, rough sanding has been completed, use a broom and vacuum to clean up as much of the sanding dust as possible. Any dust left will clog the next grade of paper as you work, and grit may scratch the floor surface. It is a good idea to wear soft, cotton socks on your feet as you sweep so there is no chance of grinding any of the dust into the floor with your shoes.

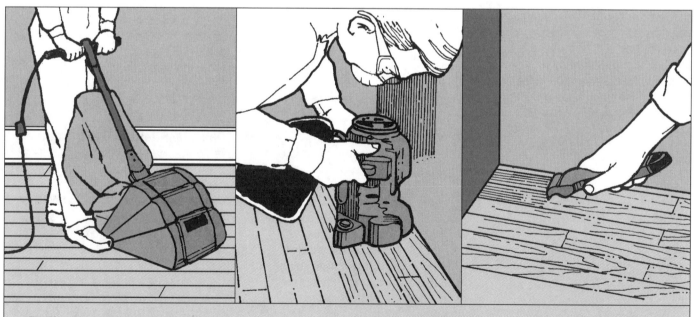

6 If you run the sander diagonally across the floor during the first rough sanding, the unevenness will smooth out (left). A small, but powerful sander allows you to sand off the finish in all but the very corners and edges of the floor (middle). You will need a hand scraper for removing the finish from the extreme corners and edges (right).

7 Medium Sanding. Load the machine with medium sandpaper and repeat the procedure in exactly the same manner as step 6; however, this time sand from one end of the room to the other. When the main area of the floor has been sanded, use the disc sander, loaded with medium paper, to do the borders of the room. Use the scraper and block of wood wrapped in sandpaper to do corners and other places the machines cannot reach, as you did the first time. When you have finished the medium sanding, sweep and vacuum up all the dust again.

8 Fine Sanding. Finish sanding with fine sandpaper. The medium sanding should have made the floor very smooth; fine sanding will produce a surface that is nearly silky smooth and absolutely even. Follow the same sanding procedures used in steps 6 and 7. Sand in overlapping strips, following the direction of the boards and always keeping the machine moving. Sand the main area first, then the borders and then the corners. Sweep and vacuum up the dust. Wipe down the walls and ceiling and finish by wiping with a tack rag, especially in corners and under obstructions such as radiators. Be sure to wipe away dust that has settled on the tops of window and door frames and on window sills and the top edges of molding. The room should be as dust-free as possible when you plan to apply the final finish. Any dust that settles on the wet shellac or varnish will cause problems.

Staining Wood Floors

While a clear finish is suitable for most wood floors, many people use colored stains to bring out the natural beauty of wood.

Choosing & Testing the Stain

Stain should be applied after completion of the fine sanding and after all the dust has been removed with a broom, a vacuum, and a tack rag. One can choose among various types for a floor, but it is important to select a stain that is compatible with the final finish material. Check the label before making your selection. Consider the effect of the stain on the wood as well. For example, stain is a pigmented and/or dye-based material that wipes on and colors the wood. Stain is easy to apply and does not hide the grain pattern of the wood. Test the stain color on an inconspicuous area before applying it to the entire floor. The ideal test area is the floor of a closet. The next best choice for a test area is a spot on the floor that will be covered by a rug or hidden by furniture.

Applying the Stain

Apply stain to your test area; and let it set. Then wipe off the stain with a clean, dry cloth. Repeat the procedure at increasing intervals so you can judge how long it should stand on the floor. Once you have settled on a setting time for the stain, use a brush, paint pad, or clean cloth to apply the stain, keeping the overlapping strokes to a minimum. Let the stain seep into the wood. Wipe away the excess with clean, dry cloths. Plan the application of the stain so that you are always working in a dry area. The situation of a worker who paints or stains himself or herself into a corner is more common than you may think.

Allow the stain to dry for 24 hours before applying filler or finish.

Filling & Finishing the Floor

Some open-pore woods, such as oak, walnut, and mahogany, require filling for a smooth, glasslike surface before the final finish is applied. Otherwise the finish can seep into pores and create a slightly rough appearance. If your floor is oak, you may want to fill the newly sanded surface. Filling is not as much of a concern with floors as it is with furniture, however. Floors made of maple, a closed-grain wood, do not need filling.

Applying the Filler

Obtain paste filler and thin it as needed with the recommended solvent, following the directions on the label. One of the most effective methods is to apply filler using

Using Special Stains

Water-Based Dye Stain. This stain has the advantages of ease of use and deep rich color, but it has a significant disadvantage: The stain causes wood fibers to lift from the surface upon drying, raising the grain. This results in a rough surface that must be sanded before you apply a final finish. Regular non-grain-raising stain does not do this. See next paragraph.

Non-Grain-Raising Dye Stain. Like its counterpart for furniture, a non-grain-raising dye stain for floors will not lift the grain of the wood. This means that tiny, hair-like filaments of wood do not come up on the surface of the boards to create a relatively rough finish. This staining feature saves time and effort because additional sanding is not required after staining. Non-grain-raising stain comes in a wide variety of colors; however, it is an expensive material. Also, it is difficult to apply evenly.

burlap. Rub against the grain to force the filler into the pores of the wood. Both neutral and colored fillers are available. Color can be added to a filler if you wish to match your floor.

Rub the filler on as much of the floor as you can at one time. Before the filler dries, remove the excess with a rag moistened with turpentine. If you do not remove the excess, you will be left with a rough surface.

Applying the Floor Finish

When all the dust has been wiped from the entire surface of the room, including the walls and ceiling, the final finish can be applied. The most common finishes are polyurethane varnish, varnish, and shellac.

Polyurethane. The urethane added to this varnish increases the durability of the surface. In general, the higher the urethane content, the more durable the finish. Application may be made with either a brush or a roller.

This type of varnish is more forgiving than regular varnish when it comes to application. One of the greatest advantages of this type of varnish is that, as mentioned earlier, it can be applied to floors with a roller, which simplifies the job considerably. You can buy oil-based or water-based polyurethane. The oil-based product behaves similarly to varnish. The water-based product dries quicker and gives a clearer final finish. Both products are available in a gloss or satin finish.

Varnish. This material creates a hard, durable finish. Varnish comes in high or medium gloss or a flat finish. There are many different varnish formulations on the market; make sure you choose one suitable for use on floors.

Because varnish dries slowly, you have to be careful to keep dust from settling on the wet or sticky surface. However, minor imperfections in your brushwork can be stroked out if noticed early. If you miss a small spot, a second coat will usually flow into and hide the "mistake." Allow at least 24 hours between coats; more time

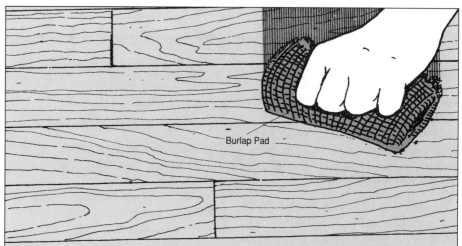

Applying the Filler. Rubbing with burlap will force filler into pores of wood. Rub across grain to force filler in; rub with grain to remove any excess.

Applying the Floor Finish. Use a wide (4-to 6-in.) brush or a roller to apply the floor finish. Follow the finish manufacturer's instructions.

may be advisable. Spar varnish may require 48 or more hours to dry. Sand lightly between coats and wipe the floor with a tack rag before applying a fresh coat.

Shellac. Although it provides a strong finish, shellac is susceptible to damage from liquids. The most attractive feature of shellac is the ease with which it is applied with a brush. Another advantage is its quick drying time, which allows you to lay two coats in a single day.

Dip the brush into the shellac, and let it flow from the brush onto the floor surface. Use a brush that is as wide as one or two of the boards, and move the brush only in one direction. You may stop when you come to a

joint between the ends of boards. Avoid overlapping your strokes from one board to another. Between applications, rub the floor lightly with steel wool. Use three or four coats for a more lasting surface.

Penetrating Oil. There is nothing simpler to apply than an oil finish. It is nearly impervious to moisture but provides little protection from scratches. Apply it with a brush, a roller, or a rag. Let the oil penetrate into the surface, and then wipe the surface dry with a soft, clean cloth. The wiping and rubbing gives the finish a warm, pleasing sheen. You may apply additional coats each 24 hours until the wood takes on the appearance you desire.

Minor Touch-Ups for Floor Finishes

If your floors have not been sanded for some time, you do not need to assume that they must be completely refinished. If a floor has been covered with varnish or polyurethane and is in reasonably good condition, you only may need to touch it up; no removal of the old finish is required.

1 Cleaning the Floor Finish. Use a paint cleaner to clean the floor thoroughly. Follow the manufacturer's directions. Remove the cleaner, taking care to wipe the floor dry quickly. Any moisture left on the floor could damage the wood.

When the floor is dry, use fine steel wool to rub out heelmarks and other obvious marks; fine sandpaper also works well. If there are rough spots on the floor, use fine grade sandpaper to smooth the rough spots until they blend with the rest of the floor.

Eliminate any rough edges that will mar a fresh varnish or other finish.

Vacuum the dust from the floor, and wipe the surface with a rag dampened with mineral spirits. You must remove all the dust. Finish wiping the floor with a tack rag.

2 Adding a New Finish. Apply two coats of a clear finish over that which is already on the floor—most likely varnish or polyurethane. Follow label directions for thinning and sanding between coats.

Once the floor is finished to your satisfaction, it is a good idea to maintain it properly. This ensures the greatest durability.

■ Polyurethane protection. The advantage of this material is that it only needs damp mopping. Paste wax may be applied if you wish, but one of the advantages of urethane varnish is that the surface is extremely durable.

■ Shellac and varnish protection. These finishes will be enhanced and protected by wood floor wax. Depending upon the amount of traffic and wear the floor must endure, you may need to renew the wax every six months to a year. Clean the floor as directed by the manufacturer of the wax product you have chosen. Apply the wax, and use an electric buffer to polish the finish.

■ Oil finish protection. The best protection for this finish is to wipe it regularly with a soft dust mop or a tack rag. Grit will scratch the finish, so it is advisable to place a small rug at the entrance to a room to wipe off dust and dirt from shoes.

If a scratch appears, you can apply more of the oil finish to the spot and rub the area back to the luster of the rest of the floor.

1 Allow full drying time between coats; thin and sand per manufacturer's instruction.

2 A power buffer makes the job easier and the finish more attractive. Most sections will need only to be polished once a year.

Installing New Base

In essence, molding provides a decorative, cut-from-solid look, and it softens corners and the junction of floors and walls.

Trim is almost always used to complete the finished look around doorways and window openings and at the bottom of walls at the floor (base).The installation of trim is not that difficult. You can choose softwood or hardwood. Cedar, pine, fir, larch, and hemlock are softwoods that are commonly available at home center and building-material outlets. As with lumber and plywood, availability sometimes depends on the region in which you reside. For example, redwood is more plentiful on the West Coast than in Florida.

You can buy standard, unfinished trim in any length up to 16 feet with lengths increasing in 2-foot increments—3 feet, 5 feet, and so on. Buying shorter lengths is sometimes less costly.

Trim is made in nominal and actual sizes similar to lumber sizing, with the actual size being smaller than the nominal. For example, a piece of case trim nominally 3 inches wide would be about $2\frac{5}{8}$ inches wide in actual size. As with lumber, this is something you must keep in mind when planning project dimensions.

Techniques for milling trim are not perfect. Trim of the same nominal sizes will have fractional differences in the measurements. It is therefore suggested that you buy all trim from the same mill lot and that you hold the pieces up, superimposing one upon the others to make sure that they are all the same size. Fractional differences in sizes can detract

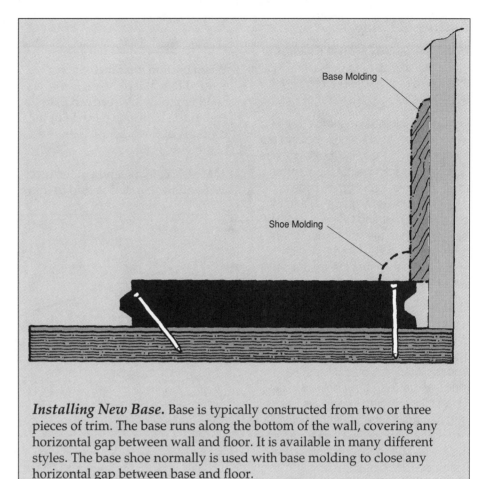

Installing New Base. Base is typically constructed from two or three pieces of trim. The base runs along the bottom of the wall, covering any horizontal gap between wall and floor. It is available in many different styles. The base shoe normally is used with base molding to close any horizontal gap between base and floor.

from the even appearance and professional-looking effect that you desire.

Working with Molding

The miter is the most common joint required for joining pieces of molding, so a good backsaw and miter box are essential. Once the molding is cut, you can fasten it with finishing nails, brads, and/or glue. If you use glue, use just enough so that the glue will adhere to the material but not so much that it will squeeze out when the piece is pressed into place.

Above all, you want to keep the glue off the molding face. Removing the glue when it is dry can affect the wood in terms of the way it colors

the finish you will be using on the molding.

Use as few nail fasteners as possible to hold the molding in position. Use a brad driver to push the brads in place, then a nail set to sink the heads of the fasteners slightly below the surface of the molding. Then fill the holes with wood filler and sand until smooth.

Sometimes molding must be sanded to remove minor imperfections. Do this very carefully so that you will not change the shape of the molding with the abrasive. Use a fine grit, closed-coat sandpaper.

Cutting Molding

Using a miter box is quite simple, but you must take care to make the cuts in the right direction or you may be left with a piece too short to recut.

For base moldings, mark the point at which it is to be cut at the top and put the molding in the miter box right side up with its back against the back of the box. When cutting an inside corner, set the saw guide so that the back of the molding (the wall side) will be longer than the front side. When cutting an outside corner, the saw should be set so that the front side will be longer than the back.

Double-check the orientation of the molding in the miter box and the position of the saw before cutting. To protect the face of the molding from splintering, you can apply a piece of masking tape down the cut. Test-fit the molding before fastening it. You can adjust the angle by shaving down any face that causes a gap in the joint—but do this cautiously since it shortens the molding.

Nailing. Depending on the size of the molding, use 6d or 8d finishing nails to fasten base. Use 4d finishing nails for base shoe molding, and drive the nails into the flooring. Nail into studs and bottom plates to ensure that the molding will not pull away from the wall. Tighten corners with two 4d nails into the wall on each side—one nail for base shoe molding.

Right Angle Butt Joints

When butting molding with a figured face at a right angle to another molding already in place, you must shape one piece to fit the contours of the other piece by making two cuts.

1. Measure, mark, and cut the piece as if you were mitering it to fit into the corner. After mitering, make a vertical cut along the face edge of the miter cut following the contour line of the face of the first piece.

2. The second cut should produce a face that fits the contours of the piece to which it is butted.

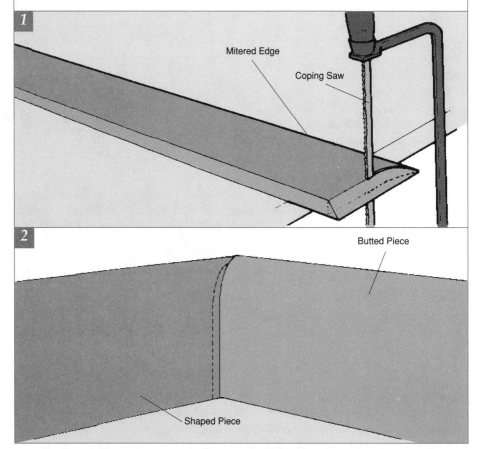

Lap Joints

If trim must be joined along a wall, miter both pieces to make a smooth joint that can be tied together with a single nail. The miter cuts are made with the molding positioned straight up against the back of the miter box in the position that it would fit against the wall when installed. Check to make sure joint falls over nailing surfaces.

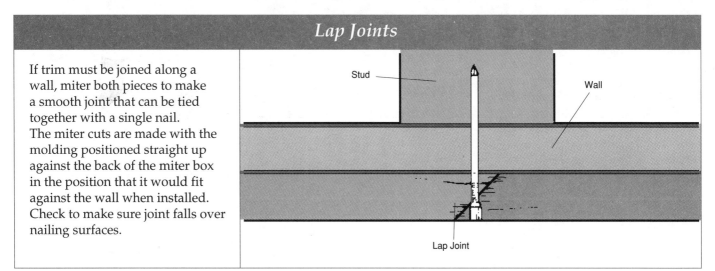

Stenciling

This process, which involves applying paint or lacquer through a sheet of cutout designs, is a popular traditional American finish. You can work out a stencil as simple as a series of letter forms.

In certain rooms, stenciling can be attractive and appropriate. Colonial and early American-style homes are logical and appropriate places for stenciling on the floors. Because the cost of importing carpeting was very high before the domestic industry was developed, many people painted their floors and then patterned them with stenciled designs.

The Principles of Stenciling

To stencil, you apply a design with a colored finish through cutouts in a piece of plastic or heavy paper. The application process is a dabbing, straight up-and-down motion. The proper brushes are short-bristled, thick and short-handled. The paint should be a fast-drying type or lacquer. Beginners often attempt to stencil by applying the material with a regular brush in a back-and-forth motion. This usually means that the edges of the design are not covered well. When the beginner discovers this, he or she then tends to overapply the paint or lacquer, stroking the ends of the bristles against the edges of the cutout. This leads to blotchy, thick coverage and bleeding of paint under the stencil.

1 Choosing a Pattern.
Commercially designed and manufactured stencils are available at many paint stores and craft shops. Designs range from simple to intricate; samples of the effect of the stencil are commonly on hand at the store. An intricate pattern may be the product of combining as many as 12 stencils to achieve the final result. An intricate stencil pattern will often look very much like a freehand design if used for a single motif.

If you have never tried stenciling, try a simple one- or two-stencil pattern. This will reduce the amount of time spent at the project and enable you to see the results faster.

Individualized stencil patterns can be created by anyone. Sketch a design on paper and do a cutout test using thin paper to see how well the design holds together. Use a soft pencil or charcoal to fill in the pattern. This will give you an idea of how the stencil will look. When you are satisfied with the result, cut out the stencil pattern. Look for stencil board at craft shops and art-supply stores.

Try to avoid patterns that require most of the stencil to be cut away in fine lines. If you feel this design is necessary, use two stencils, with one section duplicated so you can keep the pattern aligned, and create the pattern in a two- or three-step process. Cut exact duplicates of all your stencils so that you do not have to wait for one pattern to dry before moving the stencil to apply another pattern.

2 Producing the Pattern. The quick-drying lacquers that are best for stencils are available in art-supply and craft stores. These work well because they are formulated to dry quickly and not spread under the edges of the stencil. However, if you cannot find the right product, you can use other materials such as acrylic art colors.

Mark the location of the design on the floor. Tape the stencil in place. Dip your stencil brush in the paint or lacquer, and touch the brush to a piece of paper to remove excess. Move the brush straight up and down to fill in the stencil. It is better to apply the coloring agent lightly and to go over the stencil several times than to load the brush with material.

1 Stencils may be cut from coated stencil board or lightweight Mylar. Use a very sharp, pointed knife so all edges are even and clean.

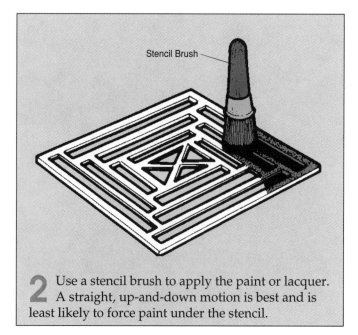

2 Use a stencil brush to apply the paint or lacquer. A straight, up-and-down motion is best and is least likely to force paint under the stencil.

3 **Providing Drying Time.** Do not remove the stencil until the paint or lacquer is dry. Then remove the tape and lift the stencil straight up. Work will go faster if you have several stencils and do not have to wait for paint to dry before starting the next pattern. If paint accumulates on the edges of the stencil or on the underside, clean or discard the stencil.

4 **Detailing the Design.** If you feel that the flat color of the stenciled pattern is not as attractive as you like, you can outline or shade parts of the design. Use a fine brush and work carefully. First practice on a design that has been reproduced on a piece of paper or scrap lumber.

5 **Applying the Finish.** It is essential that you apply a wood finish. (Usually a clear satin finish is suitable.) You will need up to five coats.

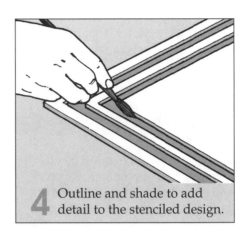

4 Outline and shade to add detail to the stenciled design.

3 Plan your pattern layout and provide guidelines.

5 Protect your stenciled floor by adding up to five coats of varnish or polyurethane finish.

Testing Stencil Pattern & Placement

You may find it advisable to test the look of the stencil positions before applying the stenciling. Tape the stencil into place and fill the stencil pattern with chalk dust applied with a pounce bag. If you cannot find a pounce bag, grind a light-colored piece of chalk in a pencil sharpener and wrap the dust in a bag made of several layers of cheesecloth. Apply the chalk dust by bumping the pounce bag over the open areas of the stencil. Remove the stencil, and you will see a faint pattern. There will be enough of an impression for you to tell whether you have put the stencil on straight and whether the spacing is correct. Remove the chalk dust with a soft brush. Any residue can be wiped away with a kneaded rubber eraser.

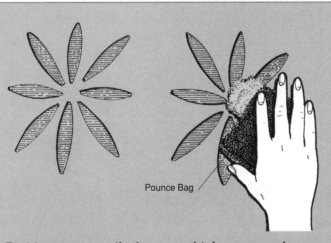

Position your stencil where you think you want the design. Use a pounce bag, filled with chalk dust or other powder, to fill the design on the floor to test the location and pattern.

Pounce Bag

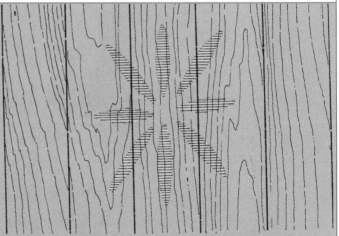

The chalk dust will leave a light but distinctive mark on the floor. Repeat the process until you can see the effect of the stenciling. Gently wipe dust away thoroughly before stenciling.

PREPARING FLOORS FOR NEW SURFACES

A floor that will receive a new surface of any kind must be sound. This chapter shows you how to repair cracks, buckles and heaves in concrete floors and how to install an underlayment to create a secure and stable surface.

Repairing Concrete

There are basically two kinds of damaged concrete floors: those that are merely cracked or pitted, with a structurally sound subsurface, and those that have buckled or heaved because of poor drainage or insufficiently compacted subsoil. The former can be patched and mended; the latter should be removed, prepared properly, and then replaced.

A 1/2-inch layer of special patching concrete can be poured directly over a flawed slab if the subfloor is sound. On a large floor it is easier to pour the new surface in sections, using form boards to divide the room. Align the forms directly over the expansion joints of the old floor. They should be the thickness of the intended surface and may be applied with paneling adhesive, which will hold them in place but will allow them to be removed after the concrete is poured. Cut new control joints over the old ones.

Holes up to 12 inches wide in a reasonably sound floor can be patched very simply with an epoxy-fortified patch. More serious cracks and large holes need more extensive preparation, including breaking up the damaged area and removing the debris. Always use goggles and gloves for such work to protect your eyes and hands. When patching large holes, be sure the wet concrete does not drip onto the good surface and remain there to harden.

Filling Large Holes

1 **Breaking Out the Damage.**
To prepare the damaged area, break up the cracked concrete with a sledgehammer or an electric jackhammer until the pieces are small enough to remove easily. Angle the edges of the hole toward the center with a chisel and hammer.

With a strong wire brush, roughen the edges of the hole and remove any loose chips or particles. Enlarge the hole by digging 4 inches deeper than the concrete slab, and then tamp the dirt on the floor of the hole with the head of a sledgehammer or the end of a 2x4. Fill the hole with clean 3/4-inch gravel up to the bottom of the concrete slab.

2 **Getting Ready to Fill.** Cut a piece of reinforcing wire mesh to fit inside the hole so that the ends of the wire rest against the sloped edges of the hole in the slab. (A few bricks or pieces of debris placed under the wire will keep it at the right elevation while you pour the concrete.) Then add water to premixed concrete until it is workable. Treat the edges of the hole with an epoxy bonding agent and, before it dries, pour the concrete into the hole, pushing it forcefully against the sides of the hole and under the wire mesh. When the hole is filled to the level of the slab, add a few more shovelfuls of concrete to counter any setting or shrinking. Pull the wire mesh about halfway up through the wet concrete with a rake.

3 **Smoothing the Patch.** With an assistant, work a 2x4 across the patch, sweeping it back and forth to screed the new concrete. Any depressions that occur can be filled with more concrete and screeded with the 2x4. When the "bleed water" evaporates and the surface looks dull, use a float and trowel to smooth the final finish. If the patch is too large to reach the center, lay boards across it and kneel on them, moving them back as you go along. The patch should cure for three to seven days. Sprinkle it with water and cover it with a sheet of polyethylene to prevent the moisture from evaporating. Check it every day and spray more water if the surface becomes dry.

1 Break up damaged concrete back to the solid slab with a sledge or a jackhammer. Clear out the debris.

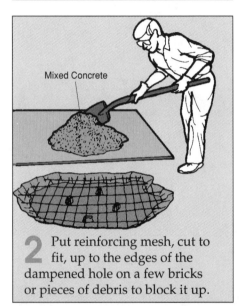

2 Put reinforcing mesh, cut to fit, up to the edges of the dampened hole on a few bricks or pieces of debris to block it up.

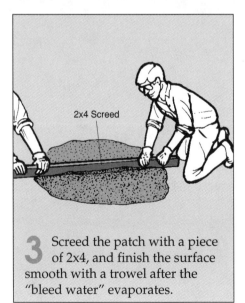

3 Screed the patch with a piece of 2x4, and finish the surface smooth with a trowel after the "bleed water" evaporates.

Filling Cracks

1 Clearing the Crack. Some cracks in concrete are not worth the trouble of opening and filling. If a crack is a hairline or slightly larger, patch it with epoxy-fortified patch. If a crack is wide enough to get the blade of a chisel into it comfortably, open it up and cut under the sides so the patching material can anchor itself under the beveled edges. Use a cold chisel and a 3-pound sledgehammer. Sweep out debris and dust. Concrete patching material with a latex binder that substitutes for water is usually considered too expensive for large patches, but it is excellent for patching cracks. Follow mixing instructions on the product label.

2 Flushing the Crack. When you are ready to fill the break, flush it out with plenty of water. This cleans the hole and conditions it for the patch so that the old concrete will not soak up water from the new.

3 Filling the Crack. Mix up the material for patching, and pack it into the crack with the sharp edge of a trowel, forcing it into all the crevices and undercutting that you have cleared out. Do not stint on the patching material; pack in as much as you can. When the crack is filled, level and smooth the patch with the flat surface of the trowel.

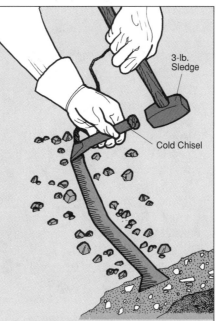

1 Enlarge a crack with a cold chisel, cutting under the edges to widen it at the bottom so the patch will not pop out.

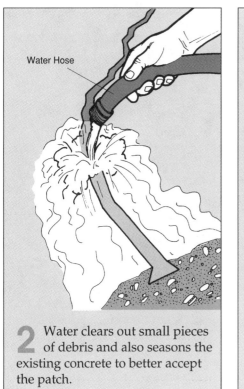

2 Water clears out small pieces of debris and also seasons the existing concrete to better accept the patch.

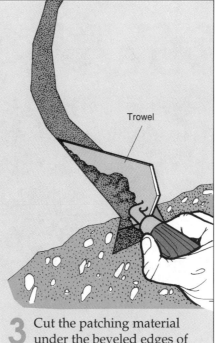

3 Cut the patching material under the beveled edges of the crack with edge of a trowel to fill every crevice.

Concrete provides an excellent structural base for ceramic or vinyl tile installation. You cannot lay tile over a damp concrete floor, however. Use one or more of the following procedures to prepare a damp concrete floor for tiling.

Check for Moisture. The best time to check a concrete floor for moisture is after a heavy rainstorm. Tape squares of kitchen plastic wrap to the floor in various locations. If, after 24 hours, you notice condensation under the pieces of plastic wrap, moisture is coming from beneath the slab. If there's condensation on top of the plastic, the problem is humidity causing surface moisture.

Waterproof Damp Slabs. If the dampness is caused by leaky plumbing or the like, simply let the concrete dry out before setting the tile. If moisture is penetrating the slab from beneath and is a continuing problem, contact a professional. Minor moisture problems can be cured with a waterproof sealer.

Check for Moisture

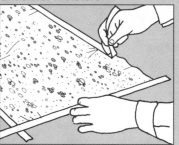

Waterproof Damp Slabs

Installing a Floating Wood Floor over Concrete

1 Putting Down a Vapor Barrier. After sweeping the floor slab, cover it with clear plastic sheets, known as 6-mil polyethylene. Overlap each seam by a minimum of 6 inches, and let the sheets lap up the wall about 3 inches. Lift up the edges of the polyethylene, and use a caulking gun to put down dabs of construction adhesive to hold it in place. Adhere the plastic sheets to the walls with a bead of adhesive.

2 Putting Down the Foam. Roll out the foam underlayment, and cut it to fit the room. Butt the joints, and seal them with duct tape.

3 Laying the Planks. Leave a 1/2-inch expansion gap around the perimeter of the room. Start the installation on the longest wall of the basement, with the tongue facing away from the wall.

4 Joining the Planks. Try to work in room-length runs. Join the planks by running a bead of carpenter's glue in the bottom edge of the groove as you install each succeeding section.

5 Finishing the Job. Tap the sections together tightly with a hammer and a scrap piece of flooring as a hammering block. Mark, cut, and install planks in irregular areas just as you would a normal wood floor.

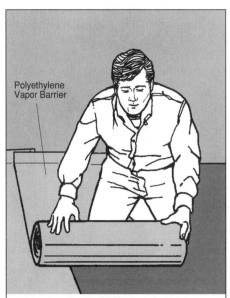

1 Roll polyethylene over the floor, overlapping the seams by at least 6 in.

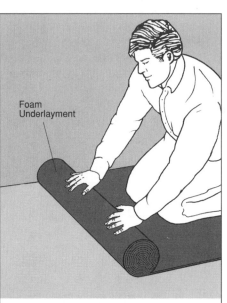

2 Roll out foam underlayment, and trim it to fit the room. Butt any seams.

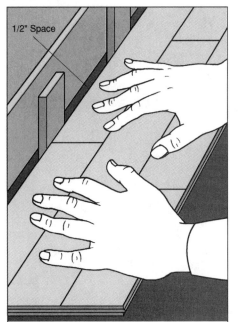

3 Leave an expansion gap of 1/2 in. around the room's perimeter, and begin laying the planking with the groove side against the wall.

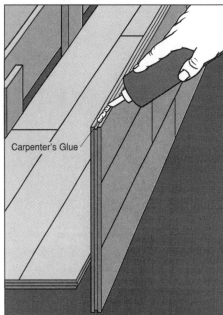

4 Squeeze carpenter's glue into the bottom of each groove, and then join the panels, tongue to groove.

5 With a hammer and block of scrap flooring, tap the joint tight along the entire run of planks.

Laying Underlayment

An underlayment is necessary to eliminate irregularities in a subfloor over which resilient flooring will be laid. Underlayment can be 1/4- to 1/2-inch plywood or particleboard. When installed correctly, underlayment strengthens the floor, creates a more secure and stable surface, and provides the smooth base needed for laying any kind of tile or resilient sheet flooring material. It also allows the floor to be raised to equal the slightly higher floor in the adjoining room. After you have put down the underlayment, patch any cracks or indentations. Add a floor patching compound to any space between panels that is greater than 1/16 inch. If you have dimpled the surface badly,

fill the pockets with putty, smoothing the patches so that they are flush with the good surface. Lastly, sand down the putty after it has dried.

Always store the panels flat and avoid marring face surface. You should, however, let them stand against the wall for some time before laying them, with an air space between each panel, so they can adjust to the temperature and humidity conditions in the room where they are to be put down. Similarly, it is not wise to install underlayment in exceedingly moist or humid weather or at times when the atmosphere is unusually dry. Underlayment should be in harmony with the ambient room conditions where it is to be laid or it may shrink or swell later.

There are four methods of fastening underlayment:

■ **Coated Box Nails.** This type of nail has a coating of resin that melts with the heat of the friction of being driven into wood. The resin rehardens when the nails are in place, holding securely.

■ **Screws.** These are excellent fasteners to hold underlayment in place.

■ **Staples.** Many professional home builders use staples driven in by a power nailer which you can rent from a tool renter. This method is fast and leaves no bulges, but staples do not hold the underlayment sheets as securely as coated nails or screws.

■ **Adhesive.** Often used by contractors, adhesive works well if you tack the panels as well.

Underlayment on Plywood Subfloor

In order to make a floor sound, underlayment over plywood subflooring must be arranged so that its seams never fall directly over the panel seams.

Remove the quarter-round molding at the baseboard. If you are building a new home, slip the underlayment into the space between the wallboard and the subfloor before the walls are finished and the baseboard attached. With grade A-C plywood, lay the grade A side up.

Be sure that the panels of underlayment always span the seams of the subfloor. If the edge of the first panel of underlayment falls directly over a seam, cut it so that it and subsequent panels do not.

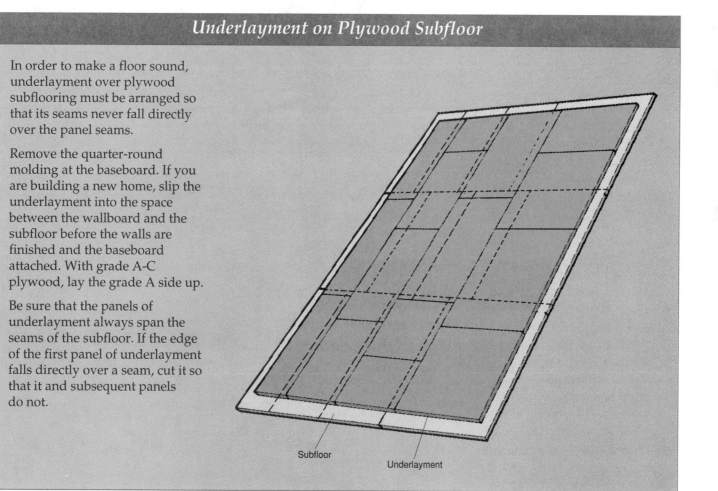

Subfloor

Underlayment

Nailing Techniques

Coated box nails are difficult to drive into some surfaces, especially the hard surface created by the resins in particleboard. When you hit the nails slightly off center, they bend. To compound the difficulty, the hammer tends to slide on the slippery surface of the nail head. One way to minimize this problem is to hold the hammer loosely rather than tightly. Doing so allows the head of the hammer to find the true surface of the nail head, resulting in a cleaner, more straightforward strike. Do not hammer hard on the assumption that forceful strokes will make the nail and the hammer blows press the underlayment firmly to the subfloor. Instead, hammer with an easy stroke and apply pressure to the underlayment with your free hand, kneeling close to the spot you are nailing. If you prefer, have a helper exert the pressure needed. Plan your last blow to drive the nail head flush with the surface. Try to eliminate dimpling the underlayment with hammerhead indentations. Dimples can become visible after a time in some finish flooring, appearing as slight depressions.

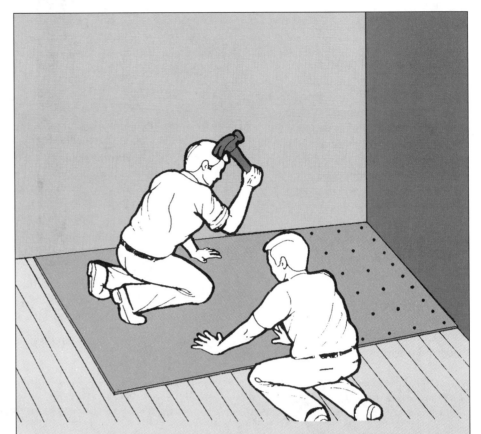

Nailing Techniques. Nailing down some kinds of underlayment can be tricky because the underlayment is hard and the nails are relatively weak. The work can be greatly eased by a helper pressing down on the sheet near the joint where you are driving a nail. If you are working without help, apply the pressure yourself.

Underlayment on Board-by-Board Subfloor

Lay the first panel of underlayment across the direction of the boards in the subfloor. If the end of the panel falls directly over a seam in the floor, cut it so that it falls in the middle of a board.

Use ring-shank nails every 6 inches along the edges, keeping the nails 3/8 inch from the edges, and every 8 inches in the field. Nails should be long enough to penetrate the subfloor but not the floor framing.

Leave about 1/16 inch between the ends of sheets of underlayment for minor expansion and contraction.

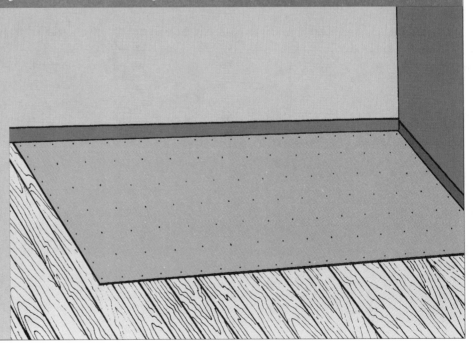

INSTALLING WOOD FLOORS

Putting in a wood strip floor is a job that requires a thorough knowledge of the process and a certain expertise in handling wood. If you are doing this project for the first time, study the procedure in detail.

Installing Wood Strip Flooring

Assuming the substructures are sound and sturdy, the subfloor must be adequately prepared to receive the new flooring. A subfloor is coverable if it is not seriously damaged. Drive down all nails until they are flush, and correct any defective decking. With a resilient tile floor, be sure the tiles are all fixed tightly; replace or recement any loose ones. If a wooden or tile floor is badly damaged, lay a new subfloor.

Concrete makes a good subfloor if it is dry. A moisture barrier—a thin sheet of polyethylene sandwiched between sleepers made of 2x4s—will keep out dampness that could rot the floor. When ordering oak flooring, judge the quality by standards set by the National Oak Flooring Manufacturers Association. In order of decreasing quality they are: clear, select, No. 1 common and No. 2 common. The standards are determined by color, grain, and imperfections such as streaks and knots.

When ordering 3/4x2¼-inch strips, multiply the number of square feet in the room by 1.383 to determine the amount of board feet you will need in judging wastage. For other size strips, ask your dealer how to compute the quantity.

To prepare the room, remove the shoe moldings, the baseboards (numbering them so you can replace them in the same sequence), radiator grates, and floor vents. Also lay a piece of new floor on top of the old near the door to see how much of the door may need to be shaved off to permit an unobstructed swing. Allow for the height of the threshold, if there will be one.

Reversing Direction

If you intend to continue flooring in hallways or closets that open off the room, you will have to butt two strips, groove to groove, at the transition point. To reverse tongue direction, place a slip tongue (available from flooring dealers) into the grooves of the last course of strips nailed down and slip over it the grooves of the strips that will reverse the tongue direction. Then nail the reversed strips into place, driving the nails through the tongues, and proceed as usual.

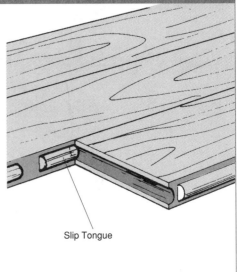

Slip Tongue

1 Laying Building Paper. Remove the baseboard and shoe moldings and nail down any loose boards in the subfloor, setting all raised nail heads. Lay a covering of 15-pound, asphalt-saturated felt building paper over the subfloor. Butt the seams tightly and cut the edges flush with the walls. Nail around the edges of each sheet. When it is in place, use chalk to mark the position of the joists.

Framing Borders

Obstacles such as fireplace corners should have a professionally finished look. This can be done using a miter box to cut trim at 45-degree angles to make the corners of the frame. You will have to remove the tongues from any pieces of flooring that will run perpendicular to the wood strips or that must butt against hearth stones.

1 Cut building paper to fit closely around obstructions, tack it down, and mark the joist locations.

2 Laying Work Lines. After you have laid asphalt-felt building paper, it is important to snap work lines based on either a wall that is square or on the center of the room. First mark the joist lines on the building paper with chalk. Next find the midpoints of the two walls that are parallel to the joists and snap a chalk line between them. From this line, measure equal distances to within about 1/2 inch of the end wall where you will begin laying boards. Snap a chalk line between these two points and let this be your work line for the first course of strips, regardless of how uneven the wall behind it may be. Any gap between the first course and the wall can be filled with strips trimmed to fit to within 1/2 inch and covered with the baseboard and shoe molding.

3 Align a Starter Course. Along the work line that is drawn 1/2 inch from the wall, lay out the starter course (the first row of strips) the full length of the wall. Drill holes along the back edges of the strips and over the joists, slightly smaller than the nails. Then face-nail the strips.

4 Nailing through the Tongue. Pre-drill holes through the tongue of the first course of strips into the joists. Then drive in finishing nails and set them. The first few rows of strips will be too close to the wall to use a power nailer.

5 Laying a Field. Lay out several courses of flooring strips the way they will be installed. Plan as much as six or seven rows ahead. Stagger the end joints so that each joint is more than 6 inches from the joints in the adjoining rows. You may have to cut pieces to fit at the end of each row. Try to fit the pattern so that no end piece is shorter than 8 inches. Leave about 1/2 inch between the end of each row and the wall. When you have laid out a field of rows, begin to fit and nail the strips.

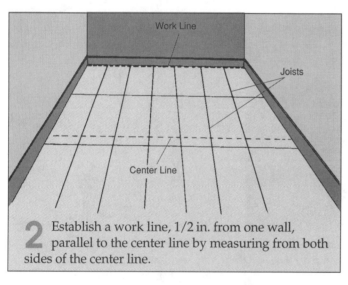

2 Establish a work line, 1/2 in. from one wall, parallel to the center line by measuring from both sides of the center line.

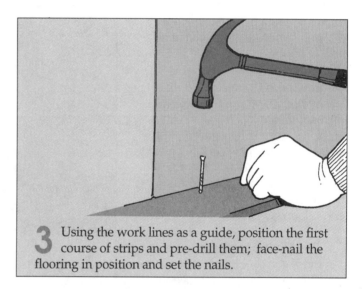

3 Using the work lines as a guide, position the first course of strips and pre-drill them; face-nail the flooring in position and set the nails.

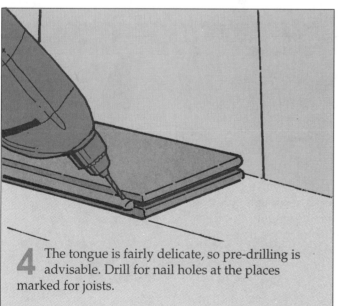

4 The tongue is fairly delicate, so pre-drilling is advisable. Drill for nail holes at the places marked for joists.

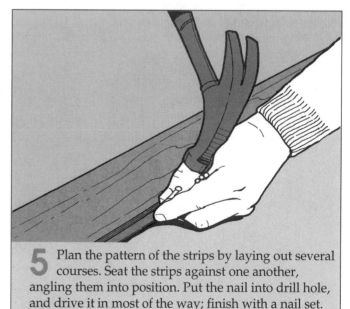

5 Plan the pattern of the strips by laying out several courses. Seat the strips against one another, angling them into position. Put the nail into drill hole, and drive it in most of the way; finish with a nail set.

6 **Fitting and Nailing.** As you lay each row, use a scrap of flooring as a tapping block. Do not hit the block too hard or you may damage the tongue. To keep from marring the flooring with the hammer when you nail, do not hammer nails flush into the tongue. Instead leave the nail head slightly exposed, and then use the tip of the nail set to hammer the nail flush into the strip.

7 **Cutting Around Obstacles.** When you come to an obstacle such as plumbing pipes, trial-fit the boards, measuring carefully. Make a cardboard template if necessary to transfer the cut onto the board. Decide whether you should save the tongue or groove. Clamp the board to a workbench, and cut it to fit with a hand or power saw.

8 **Finishing Doorways.** To finish a doorway where the new floor will meet a floor that is lower, install a reducer strip by face-nailing it. The reducer strip is made so that one side will fit over the tongue of the adjoining board. The strip also can be butted to meet flooring that runs perpendicular to the doorway.

9 **The Final Board.** For gaps of more than 1/2 inch between the final strip and the wall, remove the tongue sides of as many strips as you need, cut them to width, and wedge them into place with a pry bar. Hold them tightly with the pry bar by placing your foot on the bar while its hooked end pulls the filler board up tightly against the last board. Face-nail these last strips, and then replace the baseboards and shoe moldings.

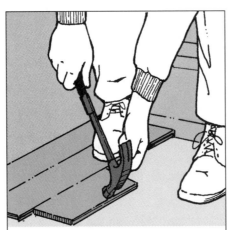

6 Fit boards together tightly by using a tapping block to protect the tongue of the board.

7 Butt flooring up to obstacles and mark the strip end. Measure from the wall for the depth of cut.

8 A reducer strip makes a smooth transition from the flooring to a lower surface.

9 Use a pry bar between the wall and the last course to wedge it into position.

Using a Power Nailer

When you reach the fourth row or so of strips, you will have enough room to use a rented power nailer. Begin about 2 inches from the wall, and slip the power nailer onto the tongue of the last strip laid. Hold the new strip in position by placing your foot on it. Strike the plunger with a rubber-headed mallet hard enough to drive a nail through the tongue corner and into the floor. Drive a nail into each joist and into the subfloor halfway between joists.

INSTALLING PARQUET TILE

Parquet tile is easy to lay and offers the elegance and durability of fine wood floors. Before the creation of wood tile, parquet floors were laid piece by piece. Now you can purchase tiles in which simple or intricate designs are already arranged. The installation process is similar to laying ceramic tile.

Laying Parquet Tile

In general, parquet is arranged and laid very much like resilient vinyl tiles with some differences, particularly its two adjacent tongued edges and two grooved edges. It will have to be cut with a saw when you need smaller pieces for borders.

It is important to have a smooth undersurface on which to lay parquet tiles. Unlike resilient tiles, which follow slight bumps and indentations in the underlayment, parquet is hard and inflexible and tends to rock on uneven surfaces, providing an undesirable floor condition.

Parquet can be set on old wood floors if they are smooth and even. Use a sander to remove old paint, varnish, and wax. Nail down any loose flooring and set all nails. If any flooring is badly damaged, you should put an underlayment down before laying new parquet flooring.

It is not wise to lay parquet tiles directly on a concrete subfloor unless you know from experience that your concrete slab remains completely dry throughout the year.

Parquet should not be installed over old resilient flooring. Either remove the old flooring or cover it with an underlayment.

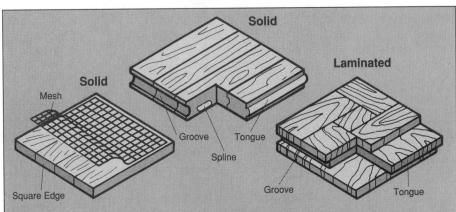

Laying Parquet Tile. Solid-wood tiles (usually oak) are made of blocks of one thickness of wood that are held together with splines or glued mesh. Laminated tiles consist of several layers of hardwood glued together.

1 Establishing Working Lines.
Mark the working lines by measuring the center points on two opposite walls. Drive a nail into each and stretch a chalk line between them, and do the same on the other walls, but do not snap the chalk lines yet. With a carpenter's square, determine that they form a true 90-degree angle. If this is done accurately, the tiles form a grid perfectly centered in the room. If the room is irregularly shaped, has various entrances, or has walls that are curved or bowed, you may want to adjust the working lines to minimize whatever visual effects the shape of the room will have on the grid. If the floor near one wall is usually hidden by furniture, make the adjustment there.

2 Making a Trial Run. Practice laying out several tiles along two work lines that form a quadrant. Get used to the tongue-and-groove construction of the tiles. There will be two right-angle edges with tongues, and two right-angle edges with grooves. If you place them correctly, tongue into groove, you will create the basket-weave pattern of the parquet floor. Alternate the grains as you set the tiles, placing the tongues into the grooves and vice versa.

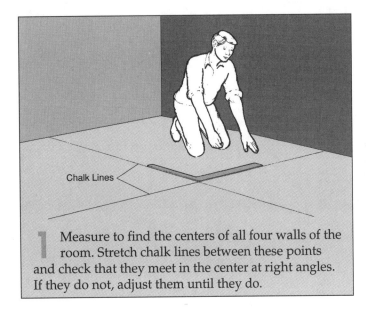

1 Measure to find the centers of all four walls of the room. Stretch chalk lines between these points and check that they meet in the center at right angles. If they do not, adjust them until they do.

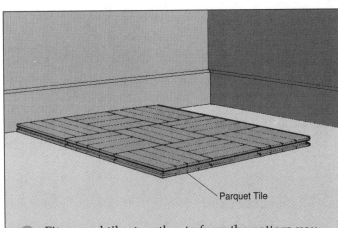

2 Fit several tiles together to form the pattern you want, and observe how the tongues and grooves are oriented. Then lay tiles along two work lines and note how wide the tiles that meet the wall will be.

3 Setting the First Tiles. Before you begin to spread the adhesive read the instructions and note how much time you will have to work before it sets. Apply the adhesive along one chalk line with a notched trowel angled at 45 degrees to the floor. Begin at the intersection and work toward the wall, leaving part of the chalk line exposed for guidance. Lay the first tile into a corner of the intersection. Align the edges of the tiles, not the tongues, with the lines. Place the second tile against the first one, engaging the tongue and groove. Avoid sliding the tiles any more than is necessary. After you have laid four or five tiles, strike them with a rubber mallet to bed them. The first 10 or 12 tiles determine the alignment for the rest of the floor.

4 Creating the Border. To make a border, align tile #2 (refer to drawing) over tile #1 and place tile #3 over tiles #1 and #2, pushing it to 1½ to 3¼ inches away from the wall. It helps to place a wood spacer of that width between the top tile and the wall. This gap is needed for the cork expansion strip that comes with the tiles. Mark tile #2 using tile #3 as a guide. Then saw along the mark. Tile #2 will be the piece to place in the border.

5 Cutting under Door Jambs. Using a tile for a guide, mark how much of the door jamb must be removed to allow the tile to fit under it. Then trim the bottom of the jamb with a saw.

6 Finishing the Job. Allow the adhesive to dry overnight, and then replace the base and shoe molding. Insert the cork expansion strip before replacing these; be sure to drive nails into the baseboard, not down into the tile. If an inward swinging door will not clear the raised floor, remove the door and shave off part of the bottom edge. Finish the floor with a reliable paste wax, and buff it twice a year. Wet-mopping or scrubbing will ruin the finish.

3 Spread adhesive with a notched trowel. Set an edge of a tile in place and drop the tile into the adhesive. Do not slide tiles into position.

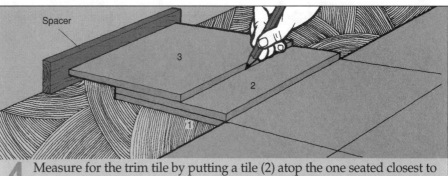

4 Measure for the trim tile by putting a tile (2) atop the one seated closest to the wall (1) and a third tile (3) atop those two and pushed against the spacer at the wall.

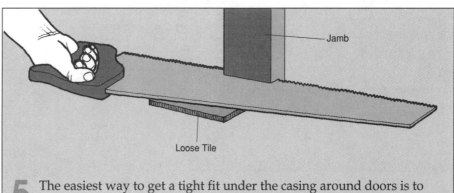

5 The easiest way to get a tight fit under the casing around doors is to cut it with a saw resting on a tile to gauge the correct depth.

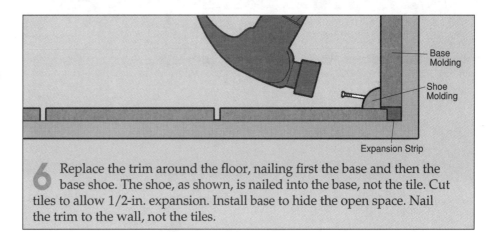

6 Replace the trim around the floor, nailing first the base and then the base shoe. The shoe, as shown, is nailed into the base, not the tile. Cut tiles to allow 1/2-in. expansion. Install base to hide the open space. Nail the trim to the wall, not the tiles.

Maintaining Parquet Tiles

Day-to-day maintenance of wood tile, either parquet squares or planks, usually consists of nothing more than dust mopping, vacuuming, or sweeping the floor with a soft broom.

Washing and Cleaning. Do not scrub a wood tile floor with water, although you should remove stains quickly, using a damp cloth. Most manufacturers of prefinished wood flooring products recommend only a light polishing with a good paste wax. Do not use a water-

emulsion wax. Apply the wax about twice a year, according to manufacturer's directions. Buff thoroughly to bring out the natural coloring and sheen of the materials.

Disguising Scratches and Marks. These can be concealed by applying wood stain with a cotton swab. Fill deeper gouges with colored wood filler. Smooth the patch with steel wool or very fine sandpaper, and buff it. Use a good paste wax; then buff again.

Replacing Parquet Tiles

1. If a floor tile becomes damaged, you can remove it. To remove a wood tile, use a circular saw set to equal the thickness of the tile.

2. Cut along the joint lines. Do not cut into surrounding joints. Finish cutting through at the corners using a thin chisel. Pry out the tongue of the old tile.

3. Then cut away the bottom lip on the edge of the tile. Apply mastic, and press the tile in place. Tap the tile using a carpet-covered block of wood. The carpet strip acts as a buffer to prevent scratches.

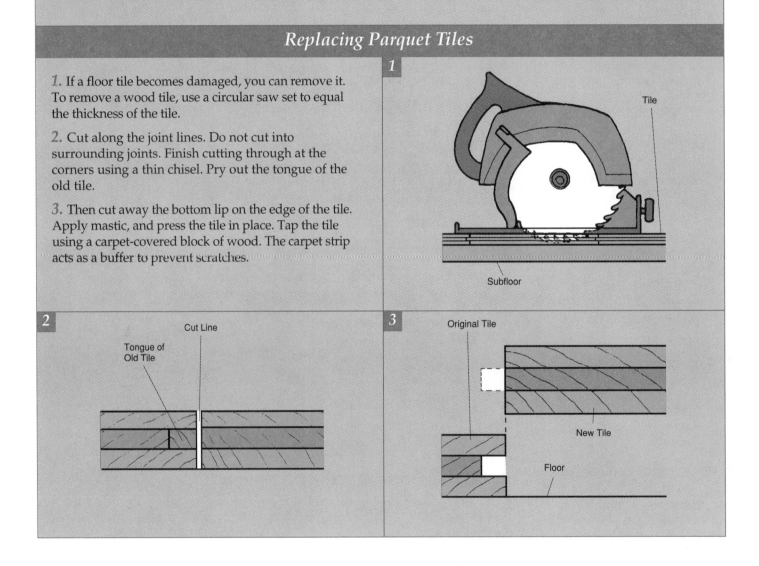

INSTALLING RESILIENT TILE

Homeowners with a creative bent often enjoy installing resilient tile in intricate patterns because it can be relatively easy and satisfying. For a successful job, however, you must plan ahead, make proper preparations, design the pattern and color combinations, measure accurately, and work without being interrupted.

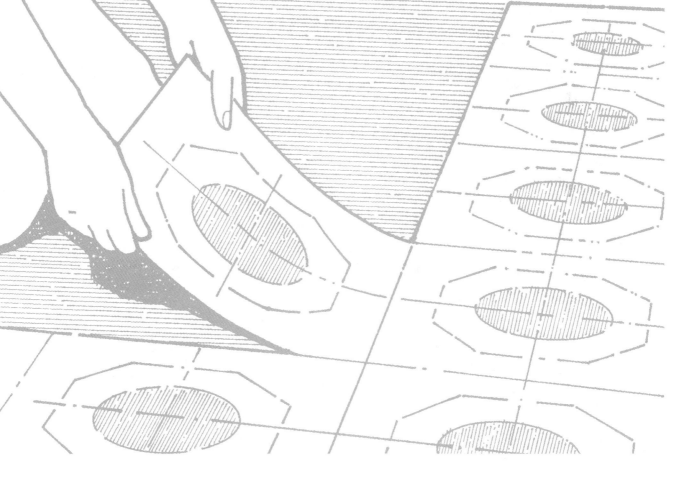

Laying Resilient Tile

A wood floor makes a suitable base for tile only if there is at least 2 feet of ventilation between it and the ground so the wood doesn't rot. If it does not have this space, you should consult a professional contractor to learn how it can be made suitable. Wood flooring laid over a durable subfloor will suffice, if the boards are at least 4 inches wide and they are smooth and sound. If there are any damaged boards, replace them. Nail any loose boards down tight, sand them smooth, and fill cracks and splits with wood putty. If the entire floor is in poor condition or if it is only a single layer of wood subfloor, install an underlayment.

Concrete can serve as a base for tile only if it is smooth and dry. If it is not perfectly dry throughout the year, it will harm the tiles. Be sure the slab is never subject to moisture penetration; test it during the rainy and humid seasons of the year. If you think it is safe, fill the cracks and dimples with a latex underlayment compound as directed by the manufacturer.

The tile and all the materials should be kept at a room temperature of at least 70 degrees for 24 hours before and after it is laid.

Plotting a Design

Plot your design on graph paper, letting each square represent one tile. If you use 12-inch tiles, you will need one graph square for each foot of floor space. A 16-foot room will require 16 squares per side. The number of square feet in the room equals the number of 12-inch tiles you will need. If you use 9-inch tiles, multiply the dimensions of the room by 1.33 to determine how many tiles to a side. A 16-foot room will need 21.3, or 22, graph squares per side. For 9-inch tiles, multiply the number of square feet by 1.78.

Laying the Tiles

1 **Marking Guidelines.** Measure and mark the center points of two opposite walls and stretch a chalk line between nails driven into them. Do the same on the other walls. Do not snap the lines yet. Use a carpenter's square to determine that they intersect at a true 90-degree angle.

If the pattern is to be laid on a diagonal, measure the shorter chalk line from the intersection to the wall. Then measure that distance on either side of the nail. Do the same on the opposite wall and drive nails into the four new points. Stretch chalk lines between these nails so that they intersect in the middle.

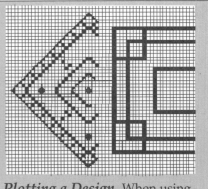

Plotting a Design. When using different colors, plot out the design on graph paper using one square for each tile.

2 **Adjusting the Guidelines.** Lay dry tiles in one quadrant. Begin at the intersection and extend them out at 90 degrees along the strings all the way to the two walls. Duplicate the color combination on the graph paper. If you discover the last tiles are less than one-half tile width from the wall, move the chalk string to make a wider border at the wall. If the last tile is more than one-half tile width from the wall, leave the chalk string where you have it. In either case, snap the string and mark your line on the floor.

For a diagonal pattern, lay dry tiles along two perpendicular lines point to point and a row of tiles along the intersecting diagonal line. If the places where the border tiles butt the walls are not aesthetically pleasing to you, adjust the chalk strings; then snap them.

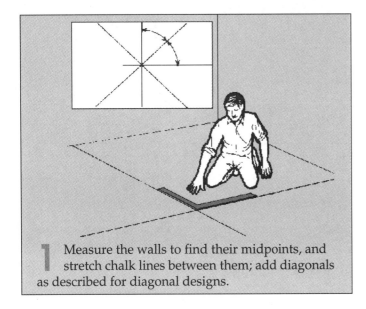

1 Measure the walls to find their midpoints, and stretch chalk lines between them; add diagonals as described for diagonal designs.

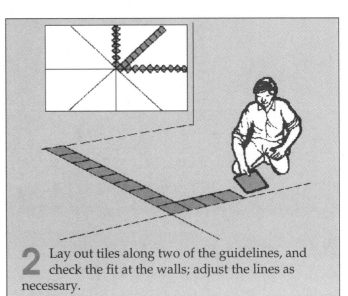

2 Lay out tiles along two of the guidelines, and check the fit at the walls; adjust the lines as necessary.

3 Setting Tile. Spread adhesive along one chalk line with a notched trowel angled 45 degrees to the floor. Begin at the intersection and work toward the wall, leaving part of the chalk line exposed for guidance. Adhesive should be laid half as thick as a tile. Set a row of tiles along the line, letting each tile butt the preceding one. Place the edges first, and then drop tiles into place; do not slide them. Set a row perpendicular to the first, and fill in the tiles between them.

For a diagonal pattern, begin at the intersection of diagonal lines and lay a row along one diagonal. Use this as a base line on which to build your pattern. After finishing a section, roll it with a rented roller or a rolling pin.

Trimming a Border

Align a dry tile over the last set tile from the wall. Then place a third tile over these two and push it to 1/8 inch from the wall. Using this top tile as a guide, score a line with a utility knife on the tile immediately under it. Snap the tile, if possible, on the scored line, and fit into the border the piece that was not covered by the top tile. For a diagonal pattern, score the border tiles from corner to corner with a straightedge and a knife. Snap them to make triangular halves to complete the sawtooth border pattern.

Cutting around a Corner

Align a tile over the last set tile on the left side of the corner. Place a third tile over these two and push it to 1/8 inch from the wall. Mark the edge with a pencil. Then, without turning the marked tile, align it on the last set tile to the right of the corner. Mark it in a similar fashion. Cut the marked tile with a knife to remove the corner section. Fit the remaining part around the corner.

Another way to cut around a corner is to use a contour gauge. This tool will provide an accurate copy of the corner. The gauge adjusts to the proper shape and allows you to copy the outline.

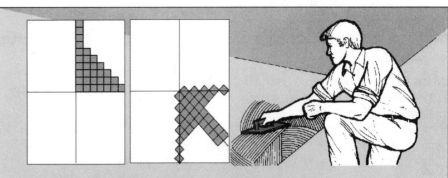

3 Apply adhesive with a notched trowel in one quadrant, leaving the guidelines visible. Set the first tile at the intersection of the guidelines, dropping—not sliding—it into place.

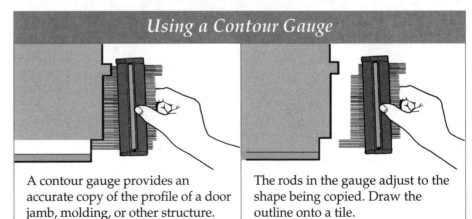

Trimming the Border. Set two tiles atop the one closest to the wall. Slide the top tile against the wall, and mark the one beneath. Score the marked tile with a utility knife and break it along the line.

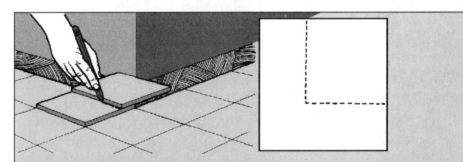

Cutting Around a Corner. Set two tiles atop the tile closest to one side of the corner to be cut out, mark that dimension, then shift the two tiles to the other side of the corner to mark the other dimension.

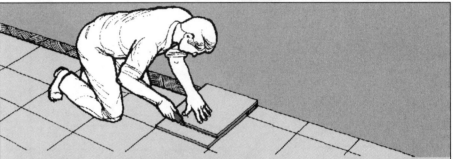

Using a Contour Gauge

A contour gauge provides an accurate copy of the profile of a door jamb, molding, or other structure.

The rods in the gauge adjust to the shape being copied. Draw the outline onto a tile.

Making Irregular Cuts

There are a number of ways to cut an irregular shape.

■ Use the same procedure used for corners, but move the top tile along the irregular shape to locate its surfaces on tile to be cut. For curves, bend a piece of solder wire and transfer curve to tile being marked.

■ Make a simple paper pattern to fit around the obstruction. Use the paper to trace it onto the tile.

■ Use a compass to draw an outline onto the tile. One leg runs along the molding, while the other draws the outline on the tile.

■ Use a contour gauge as shown on the previous page.

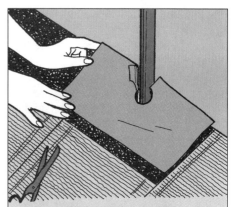

Make a paper pattern to fit around obstructions. Trace onto the tile.

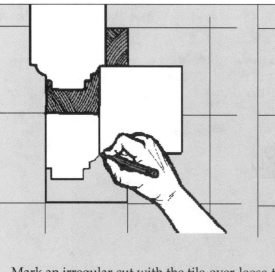

Mark an irregular cut with the tile-over-loose-tile method, moving the guide tile along the irregular surface and marking at each point; connect the marks to outline the cut.

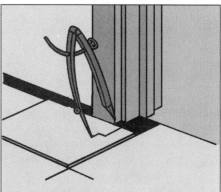

Run one compass leg along the molding. The other draws the outline on the tile.

Finishing Touches

A vinyl wall base is a practical option. Use a glass jar or a steel hand roller to roll the base. Then use a 1x2 to press the bottom of the base firmly against the wall.

Preformed inside and outside corners provide a neater look for a continuous base line.

Feature strips may be installed in between tile the same way tile is installed. First place the edge of strip against the tile, and then press it into the adhesive.

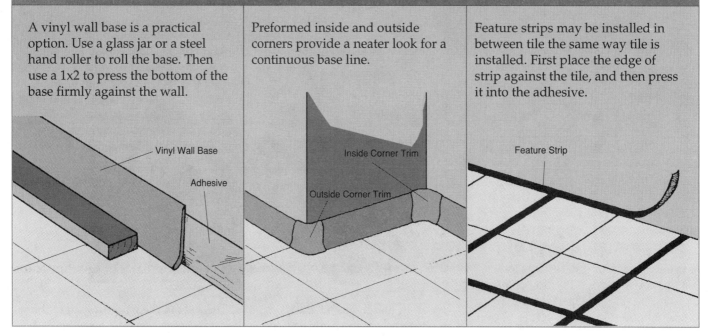

Vinyl Wall Base

Adhesive

Inside Corner Trim

Outside Corner Trim

Feature Strip

Maintaining & Repairing Resilient Tile Floors

Maintaining resilient tiles, especially those with the nonwaxing feature, involves nothing more than vacuuming the floor to prevent loose dirt from scratching the surface or becoming "ground in." Wipe up spills immediately, before they become sticky or hard. If dirt is still present, mop with clear water. Use water sparingly; never flood the floor.

Thorough Cleaning

If you have given your floor proper care, a thorough cleaning two or three times a year will probably be all it needs, except in areas of heavy traffic and soiling. Cleaning the floor not only eliminates dirt film and wax buildup (on waxed floors), it also enables new wax to spread more smoothly, resulting in a brighter shine. Things to avoid include cleaning too often and using an excessive amount of water, strong soaps, and scalding water. They can fade or discolor your floors and make them hard and brittle. Use a mild detergent that does not contain harmful solvents, harsh alkalies, or abrasives. Try to use the tile cleaner recommended by the manufacturer.

Vacuum or sweep the floor before you wash it. Dilute the cleaner according to directions, and apply with a clean mop. Allow the solution to remain on the floor for a few minutes to loosen ground-in dirt. Then mop it up, and rinse the floor thoroughly with clear water to remove any residue. Dry the floor with a clean, dry mop.

Scuffs, Spots, Stains

To remove black scuff marks, rub with fine No. 00 dry steel wool. For severe marks, apply diluted cleaner to steel wool; rub it in, rinse, and dry. During washing, rub the tougher dirt spots with No. 00 steel wool or a soft brush to help dissolve dirt film from the surface of the floor. Do not use steel wool on an embossed floor. Instead, rub the spot with a damp cloth, and rinse it with water. Remove all stains and spots as quickly as possible to prevent harm.

Protecting Resilient Tiles from Indentations

All resilient floors are subject to indentation caused by heavy loads resting on small or uneven surfaces.

Protect your floor by removing any small metal domes from furniture legs; try to substitute large, load-spreading furniture rests. The broad bases on the rests spread the weight over a large area and prevent mars and dents. Choose rests that are flat and smooth, with round edges to prevent cutting the tile. For side chairs, small cabinets, and other small pieces of furniture that are frequently moved, use glides with smooth, flat-base, rounded edges and a flexible pin to maintain flat contact with the floor. The size needed will depend on the weight to be carried. On heavy furniture that is not moved frequently, use composition furniture cups to prevent the legs from cutting into the floor.

Other chairs and movable furniture should have swiveling, ball-bearing rubber-tread casters or flat glides. Casters should have large-diameter wheels (about 2 inches) with plastic treads. Do not choose hard rubber casters with small diameters and crowned threads; these will mark resilient floors.

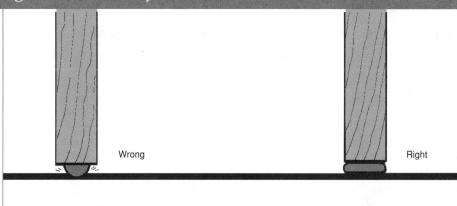

Resilient floors can be dented or damaged if furniture legs do not have the proper protective hardware. Small metal domes (left) are especially destructive. Replace improper furniture supports with flat glides (right).

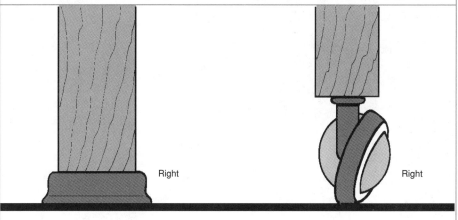

Furniture cups (left) cover the legs of heavy furniture pieces. Large-wheeled plastic-capped casters (right) finish off chairs and other pieces that are moved often.

Concealing Scratches in Resilient Tiles

Remove light scratches by scrubbing with a lukewarm solution of resilient tile cleaner that is recommended by the manufacturer. Remove heavier scratches or cigarette burns by rubbing with No. 00 steel wool dipped in cleaner. In both cases, rinse, dry and polish.

For deeper scratches, use a knife or razor knife to make sawdust from a scrap piece of resilient tile. Then mix the residue with epoxy. Press the mixture into small holes in resilient tile.

Replacing Damaged Resilient Tiles

If a tile contains a severe cut, it may be best simply to replace it.

Place a soft cloth between an iron and the tile and heat the tile. Then use a flat, wide chisel to peel up the damaged tile. If the tile is old and brittle, you probably will have to chip it out. Be careful not to damage any surrounding tiles. Thoroughly clean all adhesive from the floor, under the tile, and around the edges of surrounding tiles.

If the tile is dry-backed, coat the back of a new tile with adhesive, press it in place, and roll it securely. If using a self-stick tile, peel off the protective paper, and press it in place. In some instances you may need to use a small block of softwood and a hammer to tap in the edges of the tile until they fit evenly with the surrounding tiles. Be careful not to bend or damage the new tile or the surrounding tiles.

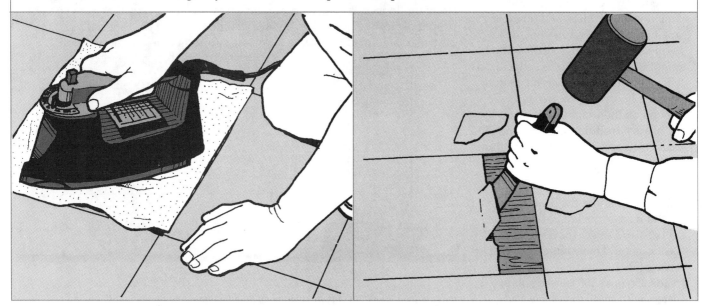

INSTALLING CERAMIC TILE

Manufacturers have introduced many new kinds and styles of ceramic tile that make it easier for the average homeowner to tile a floor successfully. Make a scale drawing on graph paper including all the idiosyncrasies of your floor plan so that a dealer can suggest the best materials and the right quantities.

Laying Ceramic Tile Floors

In deciding color and design, remember that floors with busy patterns or several colors tend to look smaller. Small tiles give the illusion that the floor is larger; large tiles make the floor look smaller. Similarly, dark colors shrink the floor visually, while light colors expand it.

Be sure to order extra tiles for trimming and in case of mistakes and cracked or chipped pieces. You should also have a few on hand for repairs.

There are several different types of adhesives, but manufacturers recommend specific kinds for their tiles. Most do-it-yourselfers use a "thin set" rather than a heavy mortar base. Thin-set adhesives come with organic, cement, and epoxy bases. Organic bases, called mastics, are water-resistant and may irritate the lungs and skin while being used. Cement bases are excellent for applying tiles to concrete or masonry subfloors. Epoxy is the strongest base and provides high bonding power. It also is irritating to the skin. Epoxy is tricky to work with because it sets quickly.

Ceramic tiles should be installed only over sound subfloors. Concrete makes the best subfloor, but it must be dry, clean, and free of holes. Some adhesives require that a sealer be laid on concrete for a good outcome. A wood base is suitable if the boards or panels are securely fastened to the joists. Remove old finishes and sand rough areas smooth. Sound resilient floors will take ceramic tiles, but resilient flooring that is cushioned is too soft and springy and should be removed.

1 Work Lines and Battens.
Ceramic tile may be laid from the center of the room or, more traditionally, from one corner. Measure the room for work lines. (See page 63.) In addition to accurate work lines, it will help in laying individual ceramic tiles to install battens made from 1x2s or 1x3s. Nail them (or glue them in the case of a concrete subfloor) at right angles to each other along the two adjacent work lines. Be sure they form a perfect right angle.

2 Placing Spacers. Inserting spacers between individual tiles as you lay them makes it easier to maintain equal spacing of grout joints, imparting a more professional look to the finished room. Spacers are usually made from molded plastic the size of the grout joints. Some spacers must be removed before grouting, while others may be left in to be grouted over. In addition, some tiles are made with raised nubs on the edges that, when butted against the nubs on other tiles, form uniform spacing as you lay the tile.

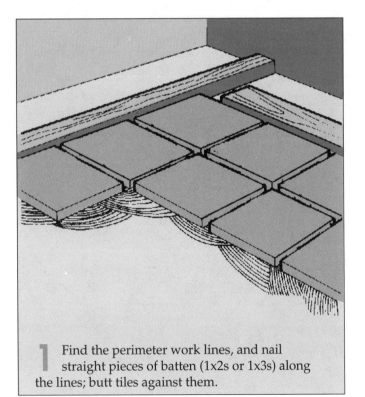

1 Find the perimeter work lines, and nail straight pieces of batten (1x2s or 1x3s) along the lines; butt tiles against them.

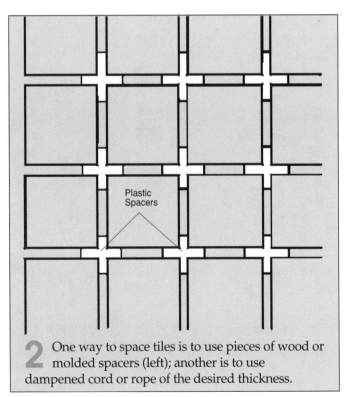

Plastic Spacers

2 One way to space tiles is to use pieces of wood or molded spacers (left); another is to use dampened cord or rope of the desired thickness.

3 Dry Run. After you have snapped the chalk lines along the intersection at the center of the room to be tiled, it is best to lay out the tiles or sheets of tile in a dry run. Sometimes, by adjusting the grout joint slightly between each tile, you can avoid having to cut tiles to border the wall.

4 Spreading Adhesive. Use a notched trowel to spread the adhesive. The manufacturer's suggestion on the label will tell you what size notch to use. Note carefully the amount of time you have to work with the adhesive before it sets. Spread about a square yard to start.

Always spread the adhesive just up to the chalk lines with enough left of the lines exposed to guide you in laying tiles.

5 Laying Tiles. When laying tiles individually, place each one where it is to go, and wiggle it with a gentle twisting motion to get it into place. Butt it up against the battens, insert a spacer, and lay the next tile. If you discover that the tiles are running out of line with each other, wiggle them into position rather than lifting them off the adhesive.

6 Bedding Tiles. After you have laid several rows of adjoining

tiles, it becomes important to bed them correctly so that they are level with each other. An easy way to do this is to make a bedding block. Use a block of wood large enough to cover several tiles at once, and cover it with a padding of felt or thin carpet. Then bed in the tiles by laying the block over several rows and tapping it firmly with a hammer. Slide the bedding block along, and bed the others to achieve a smooth, even surface. Every so often use a carpenter's square to check positioning and a level to check the bedding. Make adjustments as necessary.

3 Avoid messy problems by placing the tile (sheet tile here) on the dry floor to check for fit and spacing—before applying the adhesive.

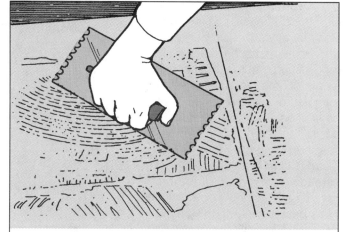

4 Spread adhesive evenly—leaving work lines visible—with a notched trowel that meets the adhesive manufacturer's specifications.

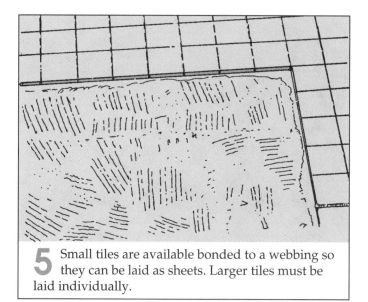

5 Small tiles are available bonded to a webbing so they can be laid as sheets. Larger tiles must be laid individually.

Bedding Block

6 When laying tile, seat the tiles firmly into the adhesive by tapping on a bedding block covered with padding such as old carpet.

7 Making Cuts. To rough out a cut (over a toilet drain) with sheet tile, cut the backing with a utility knife and remove the unnecessary portion.

To patch the areas (around toilet drain) use nippers; for more intricate cuts, make a cardboard template and trace the shape onto the tile. You can also use small grinding stones in an electric drill to make curved cuts.

8 Laying the Saddle. Cut off the bottom of the door if necessary. Apply adhesive to the floor and the bottom of the saddle. Allow for equal spaces on each side to let the wood door frame expand and a space for a grout joint between the saddle and the tile floor.

9 Grouting. Make sure there is no dried adhesive on the surface. Remove any adhesive between tiles that would make the joint too shallow for grouting. Let the tiles set for the length of time recommended by the manufacturer of the adhesive you have used. Tiles can break very easily if they are walked upon at this stage. Apply grout with a rubber-faced float or a squeegee by spreading the grout over the face of the tiles and forcing it down into the joints between them. Be sure the joints are filled.

When the surface is well covered with grout, scrape off the excess with a squeegee or float. Work diagonally

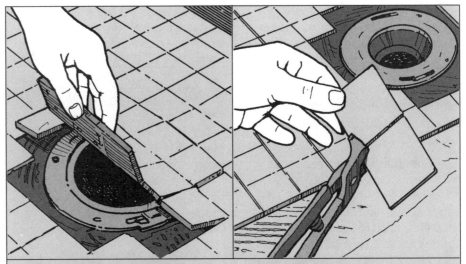

7 This sheet (left) was laid over a drainpipe, and then the backing was cut with a utility knife to rough out the opening. Tile nippers (right) cut tiles separated from the sheet for fitting around the edges of the opening.

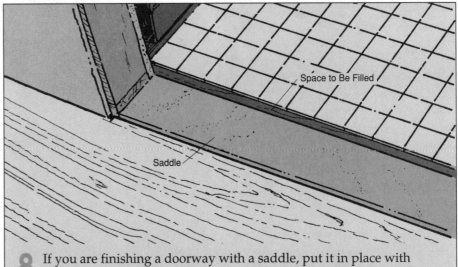

Space to Be Filled

Saddle

8 If you are finishing a doorway with a saddle, put it in place with adhesive before cutting tiles to fill the border.

9 Spread grout across tiles with a rubber float, pressing grout into spaces between tiles (left). Work diagonally across the floor, removing the grout from the surface with the float (middle). After the bulk of the excess grout is removed, clean the tile with a damp sponge, rinsing the sponge often (right).

across the tiles. As you remove the excess, check to make sure the joints are filled and there are no air pockets.

Remove the remaining grout using a sponge dampened with clean water. Wipe the tiles and rinse the sponge frequently, changing the water when it gets dirty. Get the tiles as clean as possible. Then wait about 30 minutes for a thin haze to appear, and wipe it off with a soft cloth.

10 **Tooling.** The grout is slightly rough when it dries. For a smoother look, tool it with a jointer or the end of a toothbrush. Some grouts take two weeks to cure; check the length of time suggested by the manufacturer. Put plywood over the floor to keep from stepping on new grout. When cured, the grout should be sealed.

11 **Sealing Unglazed Tile.** When the tiles have completely set and have been grouted, apply a sealer. The sealer seals unglazed tiles so they won't absorb stains, but it also is useful for use with glazed tile because it seals the grout against staining. Use a foam-rubber roller to apply the sealer.

12 **Caulking.** Joints between vertical surfaces and the floor should be caulked, especially any areas that will be subject to prolonged wetness.

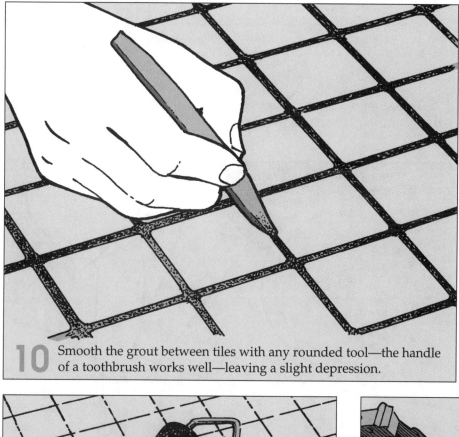

10 Smooth the grout between tiles with any rounded tool—the handle of a toothbrush works well—leaving a slight depression.

11 Unglazed tile and glazed tile with white grout should be sealed with a sealant to guard against staining. Apply it with a foam-rubber roller.

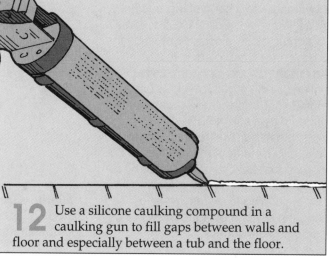

12 Use a silicone caulking compound in a caulking gun to fill gaps between walls and floor and especially between a tub and the floor.

Maintaining & Repairing Ceramic Tile

The day-to-day cleaning of ceramic tile requires only water and a soft cloth. For stubborn stains, use a detergent. Do not use steel-wool pads on ceramic tile because they may scratch the surface. Nor should you use harsh abrasives on ceramic tile. Naval jelly can be used to remove rust stains; organic stains such as coffee, mustard, or ink can be removed with chlorine bleach. Hard-water spots, such as in showers or tub enclosures, can be cleaned away with a solution of half vinegar and half water.

Cleaning Grout Lines

Household bleach scrubbed in with a toothbrush helps keep grout clean and free of mildew. However, if your tile has colored grout, test first to make sure the bleach will not affect the coloring. A non-abrasive powdered cleanser or bathroom cleaning solution often is necessary for removing mildew, grease, or other materials from grout lines. If this does not do the job, use a liquid cleanser especially made for ceramic tile.

The application of special sealers to ceramic tile adds extra protection. Waxing and buffing tile floors also will help protect the floors and add beauty. Use only tile sealers and waxes suggested by your dealer.

Buffing

The simplest way to buff tile is to rub it by hand with a soft buffing pad on an ordinary floor mop. This is called a "weighted cloth" since you must bear down on the mop to achieve a shine. An easier method (although some believe, less satisfactory) is to use a rented floor buffer. In most cases, the buffer uses a soft lamb's wool polishing head. Tile dealers carry several buffing compounds. Select the one that best suits your floor. Instructions come with the machine. The main thing to remember is to keep the buffer moving to prevent damaging the surface.

Stain Removal Guide

For Cement Mortar and Silicone Rubber Grouts

Type Of Stain	Stain Removal Agent
Grease and fats	Sodium carbonate (washing soda) and water
Colored dyes	Household bleaches, iodine, ammonia
Mercurochrome	Liquid household bleach
Blood	Hydrogen peroxide or household bleach
Coffee, tea, food, fruit juices, and lipstick	Popular household cleaner in hot water followed by hydrogen peroxide or household bleach.

Caution: *Ammonia and household bleaches should not be combined because they generate caustic fumes.*

Cleaning Grout Lines. If grout lines are affected by mildew or become especially grimy in areas that stay damp such as tub enclosure, use a toothbrush dipped in household bleach to scrub the problem area.

Loose Tiles

Loose floor tiles can be caused by several things, including the wrong adhesive, incorrect preparation of the floor surface before installation of the tile, or poor grouting. If this is the case, moisture may build up and break down the adhesive. The first step is to correct the source of the problem; otherwise the tiles will probably loosen again after you replace them.

If only one or two tiles have become loose, use a sharp knife, ice pick, or other pointed object to dig out the grout around the tile. Lift out the tile. Carefully scrape the dried adhesive from both the floor and the back of the tile.

If you have some of the same adhesive originally used to set the tile, smear some of the adhesive (using a notched trowel) over the void on the floor and on the back of the tile. Press the tile back into place. If you do not have the same adhesive, use bathtub caulking. Apply it to the back of the tile in several beads, and press the tile into place. It must be flush with the surrounding tiles. Let it set thoroughly.

Regrout the joints surrounding the tile. Once the grout has set and cured (if the directions so specify) apply a silicone tile sealer.

If you have an entire floor of loose tiles, you must start at one end and remove all the loose tiles. If the majority of them are loose, you probably are better off removing all of them. Use a wide chisel and hammer to tap the tiles away from the floor. Clean off dried adhesive from the tiles, and repair the floor as needed. In some cases it will be easier to add an underlayment rather than to patch a lot of holes. Follow the repairs with a coating of adhesive as recommended by the tile manufacturer. Replace the tiles, let them set, and then regrout them.

Replacing a Damaged Tile

It is difficult to remove a cracked tile because it is easy to damage surrounding good tiles while you are removing the cracked one.

Scrape away the grout surrounding the tile, and try to pry it up using a putty knife. If you can't pry it loose, use a small cold chisel and hammer to break the tile into small pieces and pry them up. Work from the center of the tile out toward the edges to avoid damaging any surrounding tiles. As a safety measure, wear protective glasses. To remove the adhesive from the floor, use a flat wide chisel.

Using a notched trowel, butter the back of the new tile, and spread adhesive in the void in the floor. Press the new tile in place.

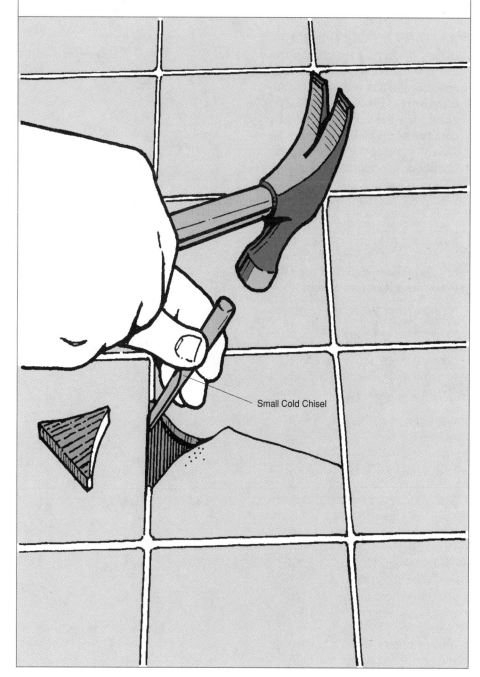

Small Cold Chisel

Occasionally a tiled area will need to be regrouted. In this case, remove all old grouting using a sharp, pointed tool such as an awl, or create a nail jig out of a 10d nail and a short piece of dowel wood.

Tools. This task requires a 6- to 10-inch-long dowel 3/4 to 1 inch in diameter, 10d finishing nails, ceramic tile grout, a whisk broom, a vacuum cleaner, a sponge, a mixing container and a supply of clean, soft cloths.

Removing the Old Grout. To make a tool to dig the grout out of the joints, drive the 10d finishing nail through a dowel near its end. (Pre-drill for the nail.) Scrape the grout from the joints. This takes patience as the work proceeds slowly. Replace the nail often, as it will quickly become dull.

As you work, brush out the joints with the whisk broom, and vacuum away the debris. It is important to keep the work clean. If you do not, you will track the fine, powdered grout all over the house, and it is hard to remove.

Regrouting. When the joints are clean and you are satisfied with the job, mix up a sufficient amount of grout. Spread this mixture over the tile. (See "Grouting," on page 56.)

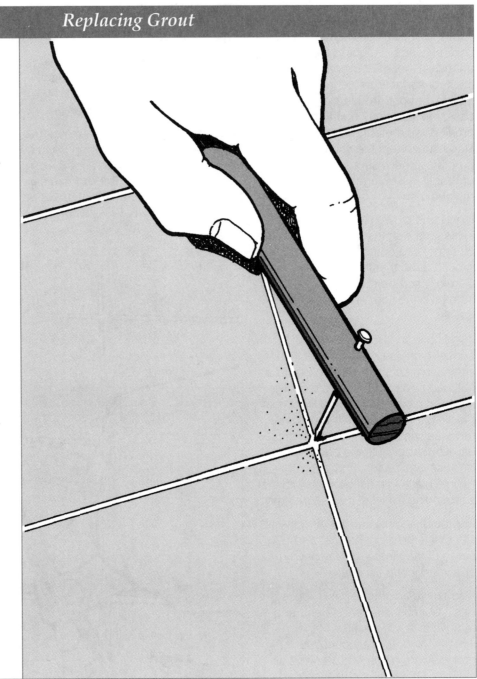

INSTALLING MASONRY

For the purposes of this section, there are two types of masonry: man-made colored brick and finished or rough-hewn natural stones. Bricks that are made especially for floors are known as pavers. They are available full size or in splits for lighter weight where structural problems would be created by the weight of full-size pavers.

Laying Masonry Floors

If you are not going to lay masonry on a concrete slab at ground level, you should consult a building expert for advice on how to reinforce the substructure that is to hold the weight of the floor plus masonry.

Brick may be laid either with or without mortar. Mortarless brick can be laid on a subfloor of either wood (covered with felt paper) or concrete. Bricks laid on wood should not exceed $1^5/_8$ inch in thickness, but any thickness may be laid on concrete. Since splits are not as heavy or solid as full-size bricks, they should be laid in mortar or adhesive to secure them. When laying bricks on concrete, the slab must be clean and dry, but irregularities can be eliminated by a mortar bed.

Rough-hewn masonry exerts a tremendous weight force and should be laid over concrete. Make sure the slab is clean so that the mortar will bond to it. In laying stone masonry, creative decisions must be made as the project proceeds. The stones can be fitted together in a puzzle-like fashion to achieve a pleasing arrangement. The thickness of the mortar will vary in order to keep the tops of the stones level. In addition, some stones will have to be trimmed to fit. The joints between stones must be approximately equal in width.

Most masonry flooring has a porous surface that requires a sealer—ask your building supplier what is the best type for your floor. When the surface is tightly sealed, the floor can be maintained simply by sweeping and occasionally damp mopping with a mild detergent. Stone floors are hard and durable, but a light coat of wax heightens the texture of particular stones and deepens their character. Not all wax is "friendly" to masonry, so check the instructions on the label.

Laying Brick Patterns

There are several patterns used in brick floors. Two possible choices are herringbone and basket weave. The careful layout required for any horizontal brick surface is obvious in the following example, which is a discussion of basket weave.

A basket-weave pattern is based on blocks of brick set on edge at right angles to each other. Each block must be of equal size. Arrange joint sizes so that the two or three bricks set in one direction equal the length of the brick.

Three-Brick Basket Weave. Begin in one corner, placing three bricks on edge. All should run in the same direction, and there should be a 3/8-inch joint left between them. The size of the block will equal the length of the bricks ($7^5/_8$ inches), which should equal the sum of the three thicknesses and the two

mortar joints ($2^1/_4+3/8+2^1/_4+3/8+2^1/_4$) to yield a $7^5/_8$ x $7^5/_8$ inch square, plus or minus.

Now set the second block of three bricks at right angles to the first block. To ensure the correct spacing, align the top and bottom brick with the top and bottom edges of the lengthwise brick they butt against. To complete the block, center the third brick between the two. Continue alternating blocks, working out and across the patio area. Try not to go back to an area already completed because you may disturb the spacing.

Two-Brick Basket Weave. If you prefer to lay the bricks flat rather than on edge, each block will contain only two bricks. Again, work on aligning outside edges to create equal squares.

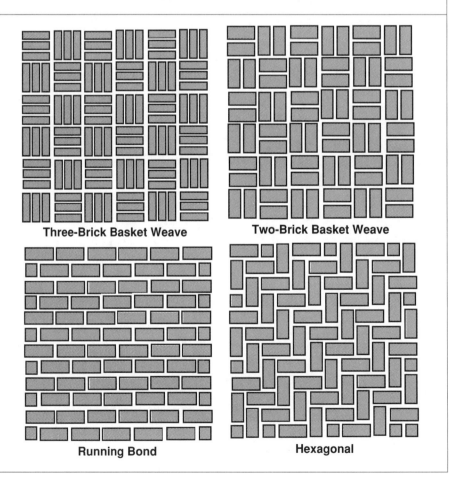

Three-Brick Basket Weave

Two-Brick Basket Weave

Running Bond

Hexagonal

Installing Brick

1 Laying Work Lines. Determine whether your room has square corners by placing tile or square-cornered masonry flush up into the corner. Stretch a chalk line along the outside edge of each tile and snap it. If the wall is crooked, you will find variations in the distance between the chalk line and the wall. A variation less than the width of a mortar or grout joint will not matter. If the corner of the chalk lines is a true 90-degree angle, snap a second chalk line parallel to the first and two joint widths from it. Do the same on an adjoining wall.

2 Laying Mortarless Brick. On a wood floor, first lay two layers of 15-pound felt paper. If your wall is straight, you will not need to lay work lines. You can use the baseboard along the wall as your guide. If the wall is not straight, lay work lines a little less than one brick length or width (depending on how you are laying them) from the wall. Lay the first run of bricks on this line. When the floor is completely laid, you can go back and cut bricks to fit this border. Lay each brick butted tightly to the adjoining bricks. You can walk on the bricks as they are laid. To make each run of bricks as straight as possible, reset the work lines every course or two. To keep the runs straight, you may adjust the joints between bricks now and then, but remember that the best floor will have very tight butt joints.

When you have finished the border, spread fine sand over the entire surface and sweep it diagonally into the joints between the bricks. Gently tamp the bricks using a bedding block. (See page 55.) Repeat this twice, allowing two or three days between sanding. Spray several coats of masonry sealer using a garden-type pressure sprayer to lock the sand in place.

3 Laying Mortared Bricks. After you have laid your work lines, lay a course of bricks dry for a trial

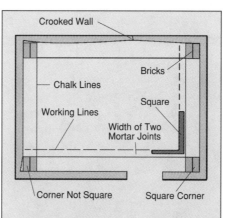

1 Snap a chalk line between outer edges of two bricks set in the corners; use square to find adjacent lines.

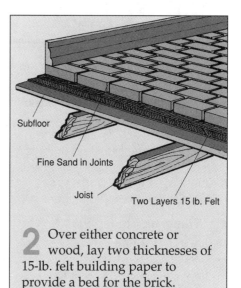

2 Over either concrete or wood, lay two thicknesses of 15-lb. felt building paper to provide a bed for the brick.

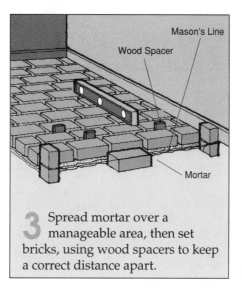

3 Spread mortar over a manageable area, then set bricks, using wood spacers to keep a correct distance apart.

4 Fill between bricks, packing mortar tightly with a trowel. Shape the mortar with a jointing tool or trowel it flush.

run. Then soak the bricks in water for three or four minutes. Apply a spread of mortar over a workable section of slab along the work line. Lay the first brick in the center and work out. Place a wood spacer between bricks to ensure equal mortar joints. Make sure the surface is level.

4 Mortaring the Joints. Mortar the joints after the brick has set for 24 hours. Use a small trowel, and pack the mortar in tightly. Trowel the mortar flush or, when it is hard enough to hold an impression, carve each joint with a convex tool such as a jointer. Scrape excess mortar from joint edges with the edge of a trowel, and sweep up later.

Splitting a Brick

You will need a kind of chisel called a brickset to cut bricks to fit along the edges of a floor. Score the brick, then break it.

Installing Stone

1 **Laying Stones.** Begin in a corner opposite your supply of masonry and mortar and an exit. Lay a couple of pieces dry to determine how they will sit. Then sprinkle the slab with water so it is damp, and apply mortar evenly for two or three stones. Tap each stone in place with a rubber mallet, and check to see if it is level with neighboring stones.

2 **Trimming Stones.** Trim stones to fit along walls and other obstructions. Trimming is done by laying a stone over its neighbor and marking lines where it will be trimmed. Score it with a brick set or stonemason's chisel. Prop the stone on blocking, and strike the scored line with a hammer.

3 **Grouting the Joints.** After the stones have set for 24 hours, prepare grout (three parts sand and one part cement) and mix it to a soupy consistency, not as stiff as mortar. Pour it from a coffee can or trowel it into the joints between the stones. With a wet sponge, wipe up grout that spills onto the stone surface. Before the grout sets hard, smooth it with a jointing tool. When the floor is completely dried and cleaned, finish with a sealer recommended by your building supplier.

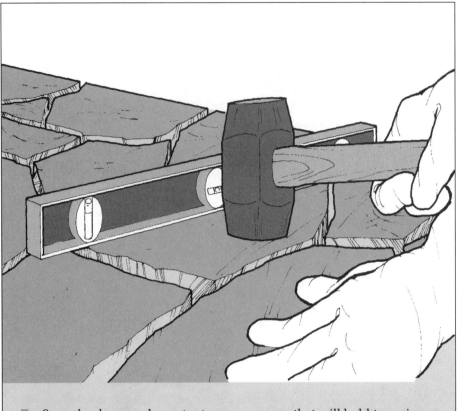

1 Spread only enough mortar to cover an area that will hold two pieces of stone. Set the pieces in the mortar and tap gently with a mallet as needed to seat them. Check the work with a level frequently and adjust the stone for level by further tapping or by raising the stone and adding mortar.

2 Score a stone along the line where it must be trimmed, using a brick set. Put the stone on a piece of board and knock off the excess.

3 Fill between stones with grout mixed to a soupy consistency so that it can be poured into the joints; smooth it with a jointing tool.

Installing Marble

A marble or other type of stone tile floor is an elegant addition to any room and the installation process is not as difficult as you might expect.

1 Spreading Adhesive. The surface that you want to tile must be clean and level. If you are dealing with an uneven surface, install a plywood underlayment.

Using a notched trowel, spread some thin-set adhesive on the floor surface. Refer to the manufacturer's instructions for advice as to how much adhesive you will need to complete the job. You will have to work on parts of the floor, rather than attacking it all at once.

2 Cutting Tiles. Most likely, some of the tile will have to be cut to fit to the wall and around corners. The problem with cutting stone is that the tiles often break along existing fissures in the rock. Cut the tile three-quarters of the way across, and then turn it around and cut the last quarter. If the stone is extremely delicate, try wrapping it in masking tape before making the cut. A wet saw with a sliding carriage and a diamond blade is a good marble or stone cutter and is available at tool-rental shops.

3 Laying Tiles in Place. Firmly lay the tiles. Do not slide the tiles into position as this will result in a build up of adhesive within the joints. Take care not to get adhesive on the face of the tile.

4 Setting the Tiles. Keeping all joint lines straight, set the tiles and the tile spacers. Allow the tile and adhesive to dry overnight before continuing work.

5 Filling Joints with Cement. Mix a batch of white Portland nonstaining cement to a thick and creamy consistency. Use a moist sponge to dampen the joints between tiles. Then fill the joints with the cement, pouring the manufac-turer's recommended amount on the tile. Use a squeegee to spread it evenly over the moistened area. Then let the cement sit for 10 minutes. A layer of dry cement should be sprinkled over the area and rubbed into the spaces with a burlap rag.

Remove any excess grouting material or adhesive before it has time to harden. Wipe the joints smooth. Then clean the stone surface with water. Tools may be cleaned with water or acetone.

1 The surface used must be clean and level. With notched trowel, apply adhesive thinly and evenly.

2 Use a wet saw, available at tool rental shops, to carefully cut the tile.

3 Lay the tile firmly into place. Remove any adhesive that may have collected on the face of the tile.

4 When the tile is straight, put the tile spacers into place.

5 Fill the joints with nonstaining cement. Use a squeegee to spread it evenly over the area.

Maintaining & Repairing Marble Tile

Daily maintenance of polished marble tiles is best done with ordinary soft water and a soft cloth. Household detergent will help clean up more troublesome spots. To deal with very stubborn stains, you may wish to purchase a marble cleaning kit that contains the proper chemicals and instructions for specific stains.

Cleaning Marble

For removing ground-in grime and even some oil and grease stains, use household detergent and a little water to make up a thick paste. Spread this over the surface of the marble in a coating about 1/4 inch thick. Cover with a damp cloth; over this place a plastic sheet. Allow the mixture to sit covered for at least 24 hours. Then remove the plastic and the damp cloth, and allow the material to dry in place for at least another 24 hours. Scrape away the residue, flush the marble with clean water, and polish the surface with a soft dry cloth.

Organic stains on marble, such as tobacco, tea, coffee, or leached colors from flowers are best removed by bleaching. Lay on the marble facial tissues soaked in a 20-percent solution of hydrogen peroxide. Cover the entire marble surface with the soggy mass. Place a damp cloth over it, and cover this with a plastic sheet. Depending on how deep the stain is, up to 48 hours will be required to remove it from the marble. Really stubborn oil stains are best removed using this method but substituting detergent for the peroxide.

Scratches

Scratches can be removed by sanding with progressively finer grits of abrasive block.

The preliminary sanding. Start with 80-grit and work up through 320-grit wet-or-dry sandpaper. With moderate pressure, work back and forth, occasionally sprinkling the block with water to help reduce friction. If you prefer,

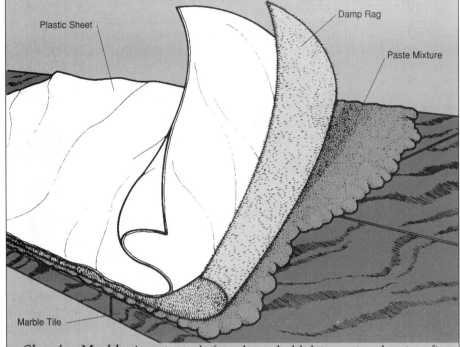

Cleaning Marble. A paste made from household detergent and water often removes stubborn stains. Apply it in layers and let sit overnight; remove the rag and let mixture dry. Scrape it away, and then clean and polish.

do the preliminary sanding with a power finishing sander. As soon as you have removed the minor scratches proceed to the final polishing.

The final polishing. First, smooth the entire surface with a 600-grit abrasive disk or sander. Then apply a slurry mixture of rottenstone and water using a felt pad on a power sander. After a few minutes of work, use a sponge and clean water to remove the slurry. Polish the marble with a soft cloth.

Small Imperfections

Remove small dull spots or scratches from a marble surface by using a tin dioxide or polishing powder. You can usually buy a small quantity of this material from monument or marble dealers. To bring up the polish, sprinkle some of the powder over the marble. Then dampen a medium-hard felt pad attached to a wood block, and polish the stone.

Once you have polished the stone to suit, spray it with a wax that is especially formulated for marble.

Cracked or Broken Tiles

Cracked or broken marble tiles often can be repaired so they look almost like new. Assemble all the pieces on a flat, smooth surface to test how they fit together. Then use acetone to remove all dirt and grime from the edges. Purchase special marble repair cement from a marble dealer, or use ordinary epoxy adhesive. With a small paintbrush, cover the edges to be glued. Press the edges together, and hold or clamp them for the amount of time specified by the adhesive manufacturer. Wipe away excess adhesive before it has time to harden.

A hole or broken corner in a marble tile requires another technique. Mix together marble dust (again, available from monument dealers) and a little polyester resin cement to form a paste. Pour it into the hole. To repair a broken corner, create a small wooden mold to fit. Line the mold with wax paper, and fill it with the paste. After overnight drying, remove the paper and the wooden form. Rub down the patch and surrounding marble, using the polishing instructions above.

INSTALLING RESILIENT SHEET

Manufacturers have developed many types of resilient sheet flooring through the years, including new materials, innovative designs, and a wide range of colors and color combinations. Many of the new floorings are durable, attractive, and long lasting.

Installing Resilient Sheet

Once you have decided upon the type of resilient sheet you would like for your floor, order it to arrive at least three days before you intend to lay it. This will allow the flooring time to adjust to the temperature conditions in your home.

Resilient sheet flooring can be installed over several types of existing flooring, but in all cases the floor should be in good condition. You can lay resilient flooring over the existing flooring if it is completely smooth and tightly adhered to the subfloor. Concrete must be dry, level, and clean. A wood floor is suitable if the boards are not rotten or warped and only if they are firmly nailed down. If these conditions cannot be met, then it is best to install an underlayment of plywood.

Prepare the room by removing all the furnishings, including the covers on the floor registers and the shoe molding along the baseboard. The baseboard does not have to be removed if you cannot do it without damaging walls or door jambs. When you remove shoe molding and baseboard, number the pieces so you can replace them in the same order.

Design the floor by using a piece of graph paper to map out the shape and dimensions as accurately as possible. Make a scale drawing to include all irregularities such as closets, alcoves, fireplaces, and doorways. If your floor is very irregular, you may want to make a full-size felt template to use as a guide for cutting the sheets. Your drawing should be meticulously done if the room will require more than one 12-foot sheet of flooring. (Resilient sheet flooring comes in 12-foot-wide rolls.) Determine where the seam will go in regard to design, pattern, and traffic flow. It is best not to have a seam where traffic is heaviest.

Installation without Seams

Unroll the flooring in a large open space to make a rough cut. Transfer the floor plan onto it with a water-soluble felt-tipped pen, and cut the flooring so that it is about 3 inches oversize all around. You will cut the excess away after the flooring has been positioned in place. Apply adhesive according to the manufacturer's instructions, taking care to note the "open time" you will have before it sets.

Some flooring does not require adhesive, while certain brands require that you spread only a 6-inch-wide smear of mastic along the edges. Other types must be stapled down or fixed with double-sided tape.

Take the flooring to the room and lay the longest edge against the longest wall first. Position the entire piece, making sure it curls up at least 3 inches on every wall.

Follow the instructions given below for trimming the floor to make it fit the room, leaving a 1/8-inch gap at the walls to allow for expansion.

Installation with Seams

Take your floor plan to your dealer and have him make the rough cuts. If you do it yourself, ask whether to reverse the sheets at the seam so the design falls into place. Use a utility knife and heavy scissors to cut the most intricate piece first, measuring so it is 3 inches oversize on all sides, including the seam. If you are using adhesive, spread it on the floor for this piece, stopping about 10 inches from the seam. Position the flooring. Then cut the second sheet so it overlaps at the seam at least 2 inches. Spread the adhesive over the rest of the floor, stopping 2 inches from the edge of the first sheet. Position and align the second piece carefully. Then cut half-moon shapes at the end of each seam so the ends butt the walls. With a straightedge and utility knife, cut through both sheets at the point where the seam will be. Lift up both halves, and apply adhesive. Clean the seam, and use the seam sealer recommended for your flooring.

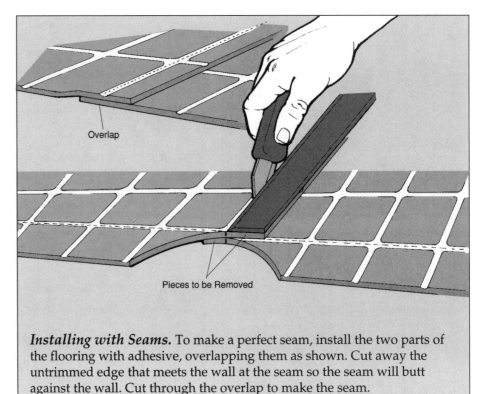

Overlap

Pieces to be Removed

Installing with Seams. To make a perfect seam, install the two parts of the flooring with adhesive, overlapping them as shown. Cut away the untrimmed edge that meets the wall at the seam so the seam will butt against the wall. Cut through the overlap to make the seam.

1 Trimming an Outside Corner. Trim an outside corner by cutting straight down the curled up flooring. Begin at the top edge and cut to where the wall and floor meet.

2 Trimming an Inside Corner. Trim an inside corner by cutting the excess flooring away with increasingly lower diagonal cuts on each side of the corner. Gradually these cuts should produce a wide enough split for the corner to wedge through and the flooring to lie flat around it.

3 Trimming Along Walls. Remove the curled up flooring at the walls by pressing it down with a long 20- to 24-inch piece of 2x4. Press the flooring into the right angle where the wall and floor meet until it begins to develop a crease at the joint. Then position a heavy metal straightedge into this crease and cut along the wall with a utility knife, leaving a 1/8-inch gap between the edge of the flooring and the wall. This is necessary for the material to expand without buckling.

4 Cutting Under a Door Jamb. The best way to have the flooring meet a door jamb is to cut away a portion of the jamb at the bottom so that the flooring will slide under it. Trim the flooring to match the angles and corners of the door jamb, overcutting about 1/2 inch for the edge to slip under the jamb.

5 Finishing the Job. Avoid damaging the finish by cleaning the flooring with a solvent that has been recommended by the manufacturer. It is important to clean up any adhesive that may have spilled or oozed up onto the surface. Then roll the flooring so that it sets firmly and flatly in the adhesive. You can use a rented linoleum roller (for the center) and a J-roller (for the edges), or lean heavily on a rolling pin and work your way across the floor. Start at the center of the room and roll firmly to remove air bubbles. After the floor has been cleaned and rolled, replace the baseboard and the shoe molding.

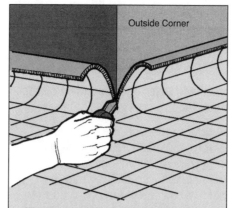

Outside Corner

1 To trim an outside corner, start at the top of the flooring where it overlaps the corner; cut down to floor.

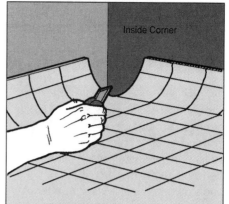

Inside Corner

2 To trim an inside corner, cut the flooring in V-shaped sections down the corner until the flooring can lie flat.

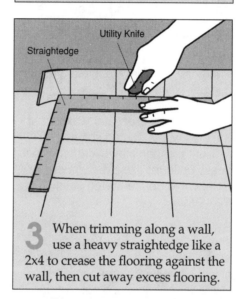

Straightedge   Utility Knife

3 When trimming along a wall, use a heavy straightedge like a 2x4 to crease the flooring against the wall, then cut away excess flooring.

4 Cut under a door jamb as shown, resting the saw on a piece of new flooring.

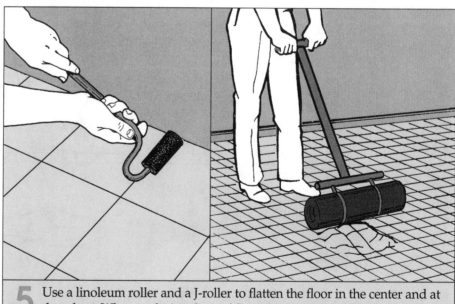

5 Use a linoleum roller and a J-roller to flatten the floor in the center and at the edges. When replacing the molding, do not nail it to flooring so the flooring will be free to shrink and expand slightly without buckling.

Maintaining Resilient Floors

Maintaining a resilient sheet floor, especially those with the non-waxing feature, involves nothing more than vacuuming the floor to prevent loose dirt from scratching the surface and from becoming "ground in." Wipe up spills immediately, before they become sticky or hard. If dirt accumulation is still present after sweeping, mop with clear water. Use water sparingly; never flood the floor.

Thorough Cleaning

If you have given your floor daily care and kept it polished, a thorough cleaning two or three times a year will probably be all it needs, except in areas of heavy traffic and soiling such as a kitchen or a hallway. Cleaning the floor thoroughly not only eliminates dirt film and wax buildup, it also enables new wax to spread more evenly and smoothly, resulting in a brighter shine. Avoid cleaning too often and do not use too much water. Also, do not use strong detergents or scalding water. They can fade or discolor your floors and make them hard and brittle. Oil-based cleaners and cleaners containing caustics, harsh soaps, and powders, or solvents such as gasoline, kerosene, naphtha, turpentine, and benzene, as well as oil-base cleaners, can damage resilient floors and should not be used. Instead, use a mild detergent or cleaner that does not contain harmful solvents, harsh alkalies, or abrasives. Try to use the cleaner that is recommended by the manufacturer of the resilient floor.

Vacuum or sweep the floor just before you wash it. Dilute the cleaner according to directions, and apply the solution with a clean mop or cloth. Allow the cleaning solution to remain on the floor for a few minutes to loosen ground-in dirt. Then mop it up; and rinse the floor thoroughly with clear water to remove any residue. Dry with a clean, dry mop.

Removing Old Wax Buildups

Using too much wax produces areas where the wax film discolors after a number of waxings. Most waxes recommended today by floor manufacturers are water waxes that wash off with a diluted solution of resilient cleaner. However, to remove heavy buildup, use No. 00 steel wool dipped in a concentrated solution of tile cleaner.

Avoid harmful coatings such as shellac, varnish, and plastic finishes, as well as multiple coatings of acrylic finishes that can permanently damage your floor. Do not use an oil mop. It will streak the wax and produce a sticky, dirt-catching film.

Scuffs, Spots, Stains

To remove black scuff marks, rub with a fine No. 00 dry steel wool. For severe marks, apply a diluted solution of resilient cleaner to steel wool; rub in, rinse, and dry.

During washing, rub the hard-to-handle dirt spots with No. 00 steel wool or a soft brush to help dissolve dirt film from the surface of the floor. Do not use steel wool on an embossed floor. Instead, rub the spot with a mild household cleaner on a damp cloth. Then rinse with clear water. Remove all stains and spots as quickly as possible to prevent permanent harm.

Waxing & Polishing

Depending on the type of floor and the methods recommended by the manufacturer, your resilient floor may need some waxing in order to prolong its life and enhance its beauty. In other cases this job may be optional.

A resilient floor is ready for waxing when it begins to look so dull from wet mopping and traffic that buffing does not restore its sheen. Apply the wax only after thoroughly cleaning the floor surface. If you choose, apply wax only to the traffic areas where the existing coating has become worn. Buff the floor first to help fresh wax blend with existing wax.

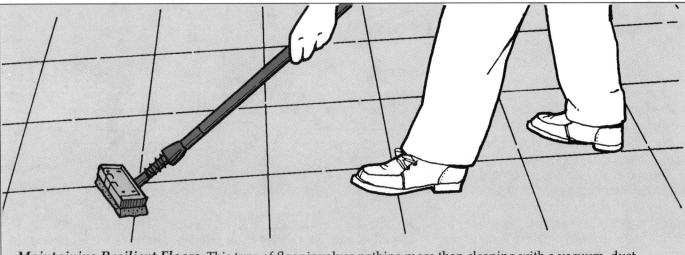

Maintaining Resilient Floors. This type of floor involves nothing more than cleaning with a vacuum, dust mop, or sponge mop with floor cleaner. Those with the "no-wax" feature are especially easy to maintain.

INSTALLING CARPET

There are two types of wall-to-wall carpeting. Standard wall-to-wall carpeting is installed on a pad and secured to tackless strips around the perimeter of the room after stretching it. Cushion-backed carpeting is laid in latex or fastened with double-faced tape. It is easier to lay and is less expensive than conventional carpeting, but it generally will not last as long.

Installing Standard Wall-to-Wall Carpeting

Before ordering the carpeting, prepare a scale drawing on graph paper letting each square equal one foot. Mark all doors, alcoves, obstacles and other unique features of the room you intend to carpet. The more accurately you make the scale drawing, the easier for your carpet dealer to recommend the type and amount you need.

If you cannot carpet your entire room with one piece, you will have to allow for a seam. Seams are weak spots in the carpet and should not be placed where traffic flow is heaviest. Some seams are visible and, if possible, should be laid away from the primary visual focus in the room. Seams are less visible when they run parallel to light rays and should, therefore, run toward the room's primary source of light which is usually the wall with windows.

If your carpeting has a pattern and will need to be seamed, you will have to buy additional carpeting so you can match the pattern when cutting it for seaming and fitting. The salesperson at the store will help you with these arrangements.

Prepare the subfloor before laying carpeting by nailing down loose boards, fixing squeaks, and replacing any particularly rotten or damaged boards. If you intend to lay carpet on concrete, the concrete must be dry and not subject to sweating. If the slab gets damp, cover it with a sealer.

Remove the shoe molding from the baseboards. Most rooms with wall-to-wall carpeting dispense with shoe molding altogether, but save it in case you decide later that the carpet will look better with it.

For this work you will need to rent two tools for stretching the carpet: a knee-kicker and a power stretcher, available at your carpet dealer. You also may want to rent a carpet cutter.

1 Tackless Strips and Binder Bars. Install tackless strips to the perimeter of the room with the tacks facing the walls. Cut them with heavy-duty shears and nail them down a distance from the wall equal to two-thirds the thickness of the carpet. Use a cardboard or wooden spacer to place the strips evenly. A tack hammer should be used unless you are laying them over ceramic tile, in which case apply them with contact cement. Attach binder bars, or standard metal edging, in doorways and other places where the carpeting ends without a wall. Binder bar in a doorway should be situated directly under the closed door.

2 Fitting the Pad. Cut the padding so that it covers the entire floor. Butt pieces evenly at any seams. If it has a waffle pattern, that side goes up. Staple the padding at 6-inch intervals around the perimeter of the room and any other places where it might slip. Ask a carpet dealer what he suggests for non-wooden floors.

3 Trimming the Pad. After you have fastened the padding securely around the room, trim the overlap with a sharp utility knife just along the inside of the tackless strip. Leave a 1/8- to 1/4-inch gap between the tackless strip and the pad. If the padding is urethane or rubber, tilt the knife slightly away from the wall to create a beveled edge to prevent the pad from climbing.

4 Making Rough Cuts. Roll out the carpet in a clean, dry, flat area. Measure carefully, allowing at least 3 inches overlap for the perimeter of the room and for any seams. Cut-pile carpeting should be cut from the back. First, notch the ends where the cut will begin and stop; then fold the carpet over and make chalklines on the back between the notches. Cut along the line with a utility or carpet knife, taking care to cut only the backing. If you have loop-pile carpeting, cut it from the front. Snap the chalk line and cut with a utility knife.

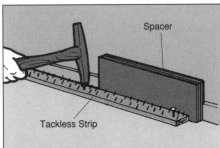

1 Attach tackless strips 2/3 the thickness of the carpeting away from the wall, with the nails facing the wall.

2 The pad should cover the entire floor, overlapping the tackless strips around the walls; butt pieces to fill the area.

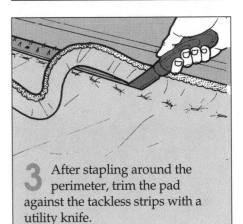

3 After stapling around the perimeter, trim the pad against the tackless strips with a utility knife.

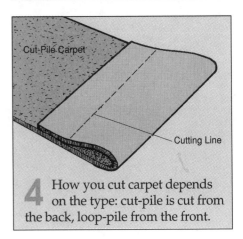

4 How you cut carpet depends on the type: cut-pile is cut from the back, loop-pile from the front.

5 **Seaming the Carpet.** To cut a seam, place one piece of carpeting over the other so the overlap is about 1 inch. Use the top piece as a guide to cut the bottom piece.

Make sure the two pieces butt tightly. Then insert a length of hot-melt seaming tape halfway under one piece of carpet. Make sure the adhesive side is up and the printed center is aligned with the edge of the carpet. Warm up a seaming iron to 250° F.

Hold back one edge of the carpet and slip the seaming iron under the edge of the other piece. Hold it on the tape for about 30 seconds. Then slide it slowly along the tape while you press both halves of the carpet down behind it onto the heated adhesive. Go slowly and be sure the two edges are butting. If not, pull them together and place a heavy object on them until they have time to bond to the tape. Let the seam set.

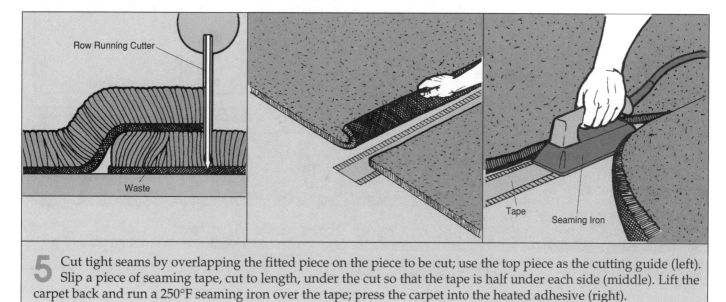

5 Cut tight seams by overlapping the fitted piece on the piece to be cut; use the top piece as the cutting guide (left). Slip a piece of seaming tape, cut to length, under the cut so that the tape is half under each side (middle). Lift the carpet back and run a 250°F seaming iron over the tape; press the carpet into the heated adhesive (right).

6 **Stretching the Carpet.** Using a knee-kicker, walk around the room and shift the carpet so it lies smoothly. Trim the edge to overlap the tackless strip by 1 or 2 inches. Make incisions for corners and cut around grates and other obstacles. Place the knee-kicker about 1 inch from the tackless strip, and at a slight angle to the wall. Bump it with your knee so it moves the carpet and hooks it on the strip.

Experiment with the power stretcher to learn how much "bite" is needed to grip the carpet and stretch it sufficiently. Pull the carpet taut with a minimum of force so it does not tear.

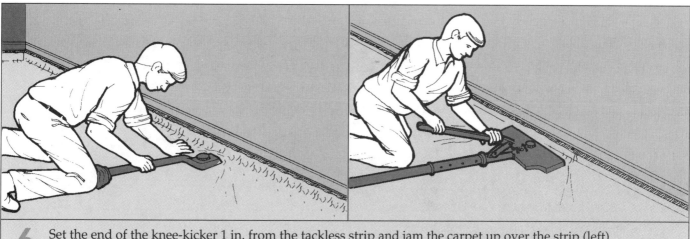

6 Set the end of the knee-kicker 1 in. from the tackless strip and jam the carpet up over the strip (left). A power stretcher needs enough "bite" to move the carpet (right), but must not tear the carpet.

7 Stretching Sequence. The drawing on the right shows the correct sequence for stretching and hooking the carpet onto the tackless strip. Follow it as you work to find the correct placements for the knee-kicker and power stretcher. You will use two techniques: hooking the corners and edges with the knee-kicker and stretching.

1) Hook corner A.

2) Stretch toward B and hook.

3) Hook edge A-B while keeping tension on corner B.

4) Stretch toward C and hook.

5) Hook edge A-C while keeping tension on corner C.

6) Stretch toward D and hook.

7) Hook edge C-D while keeping tension on corner D.

8) Stretch toward edge B-D and hook.

Check the carpet to make sure it is evenly stretched. If the seams or the pattern are distorted, unhook the carpet and restretch it.

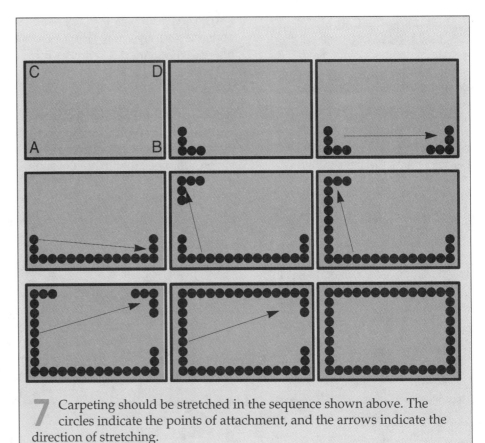

7 Carpeting should be stretched in the sequence shown above. The circles indicate the points of attachment, and the arrows indicate the direction of stretching.

8 Finishing the Job. The last step is to trim the carpeting between the wall and the tackless strip. Use a rented wall trimmer to make the job easy. If you cannot get one, a utility knife will do. First, adjust the trimmer to the thickness of the carpet. Slice downward into the carpeting at a 45-degree angle, leveling it out when you reach the floor. Leave just enough edging to tuck down into the gap between the strip and the wall. Make cuts in corners and around obstacles with a utility knife.

Use a putty knife, trowel, or screwdriver to push the edge of the carpet into the gully between the tackless strip and the wall. If the carpet edge bunches up and creates an unsightly bulge, trim it a bit to make it shorter.

The final step is to clamp the carpet to the binder bars at the doorways and any place you have installed them. Trim the carpet with a utility knife so it will fit under the binder bar. Tuck it in under the metal lip. Then with a block of wood and a hammer, gently tap the lip down over the carpet edge so that it holds firmly.

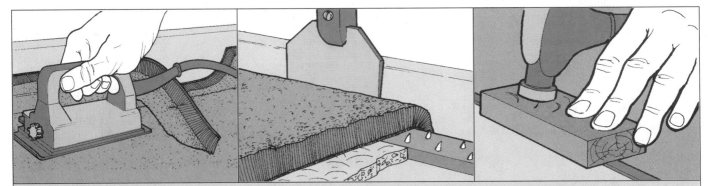

8 Cut the carpet at the wall with a rented wall trimmer or a utility knife if a trimmer is not available. Leave enough carpet to be tucked against the wall (left). Push the carpet down with a screwdriver or putty knife between the tackless strip and the wall (middle). Slip the carpet into binder bars at doorways, and close bars with gentle taps on a wood block (right).

Installing Cushion-Backed Carpet

Foam-backed or cushion-backed carpeting is a do-it-yourselfer's dream product. It is easy to measure, seam, and install over most any floor surface and provides beauty and durability at an affordable cost.

Foam-back carpeting is easier to put down than the more conventional carpeting products that require padding and special fastening techniques. Foam-back carpeting is fastened to the floor with adhesive or double-faced tape, rather than with tackless strips. The carpet padding is built into the carpeting, and does not have to be stretched at sidewalls and corners with a knee-kicker and power-stretcher device.

Carpeting stairs with foam-back carpeting is not recommended by manufacturers.

One positive feature of foam-back carpet is that the flooring over which it will be installed does not have to be specially prepared. However, there are a couple of rules, which vary depending upon the existing surface, that should be followed.

Over Wood Floors. If you will carpet over strip wood floors or subflooring (such as plywood), drive any exposed nailheads below the surface of the floor with a hammer and nailset. If the flooring has cracks 1/8-inch or wider, fill the cracks with water putty, trowel the patch smooth, and then sand the patch when dry with medium grit sandpaper stretched over a sanding block. Smooth extra rough floors with a power sander.

Over Concrete Floors. Foam-back carpeting may be installed over concrete floors, if the concrete is not subject to dampness. If the floor is new, the concrete must cure for a period of time before any type of carpeting is installed. When in doubt about moisture, the slab should be tested.

Upturn a regular water glass on the concrete floor and seal its rim with a rope of putty. The joint between the glass and the concrete should be airtight. Let the glass set for 48 hours. If moisture condenses inside the glass during this period, the floor is too damp to lay carpeting. It could be that water is seeping in through the foundation wall at the joint between the foundation and the floor slab or that the gutters and downspouts on the house are not draining away the water properly. Make any necessary repairs. Then give the floor the glass test once again.

Over Resilient Floors. If the floor is covered with resilient tile or sheet material, you can carpet over it if it is firmly bonded to the floor. If not, the flooring will have to be removed.

Also, if you will be gluing the carpet down, the resilient floor adhesive must be removed.

You can remove the old covering with a flat tiling spade, ice scraper, or regular stiff scraper. Remove old adhesive with a commercial solvent or by sanding and vacuuming.

Remove all wax, and clean the resilient flooring before installing the carpeting.

Over Ceramic Tile Floors. If you are going to cover this type of floor, the tiles must be firmly bonded and grout lines should be filled with a good grade of latex-based flashing compound.

Over Terrazzo Floors. Remove all sealers and wax before you spread adhesive or use double-faced tape.

The Rough Cuts

Unroll the carpeting in the room in which it will be installed. Let the carpeting adjust to the humidity for 8 hours or so.

Use the graph-paper sketch you made and a tape measure, to measure and mark the carpeting for cutting and fitting. As you make these marks, leave about 2 inches of overlap at the edges of the room. Also leave about 2 inches of overlap at the points where the carpeting will be seamed.

Double-check all of your measurements. Then check the measurements one more time.

If the carpeting is patterned, you will have to arrange it for any matching cuts at this time.

Be sure that the pile of separate pieces of carpeting will run in the same direction.

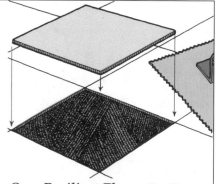

Over Wood Floors. Patch holes and wide cracks in wood floors with floor patching. Then sand it smooth and flush with the flooring surface. Set all nail heads below the floor's surface.

Over Resilient Floors. Resilient tile and sheet flooring must be firmly bonded to the subfloor for carpeting overlay. Reset any loose tiles with adhesive. Clean the floor removing wax, grease, and dirt.

Laying the Carpeting

Using the sketch, position the carpeting where it will be fastened to the floor—either with adhesive or double-face tape.

1 Aligning the Carpeting. If the carpeting has to be seamed, snap a chalk line at the point on the floor where the seam will be located. All foam-back carpeting is cut from the face, not from the back. Match the edge of the carpeting with the chalk line. It must fit perfectly. Then pull the adjoining piece of carpeting over the first piece set accurately against the chalk line. Work carefully so you do not jiggle the first piece of carpeting out of alignment.

2 Spreading the Adhesive. The adjoining piece of carpeting should overlap the first piece 1/4 inch. Be sure to match any pattern at this time.

Fold or roll back both pieces of carpeting. Then apply an even coat of foam-back adhesive to the floor along the chalk line. The adhesive should be smooth and even—not bunched or lumped. Now roll one piece of carpeting into the adhesive so the edge of it matches the chalk line perfectly. Use your hands and fingers to work the carpet backing into the adhesive and to remove any air bubbles under the carpeting.

3 Overlapping the Pieces. Do the same with the adjoining piece of carpeting. It will, of course, overlap the first piece by 1/4 inch.

4 Applying Seaming Fluid. Very carefully, apply the seaming fluid to the first piece of carpeting along the edge of the rubber-like foam backing. This is critical. Make sure that the adhesive bead is the same height as the backing. Do not get the adhesive on the pile. This adhesive comes in a

tube with a nozzle. You can cut a V notch in the nozzle with a razor blade so you can squeeze out the adhesive. Match the height of the backing with the razor cut in the nozzle.

5 Working Out the Bulges. Once you have applied the seaming adhesive, pull the second piece of carpeting back slightly so it butts the carpeting already set on the floor. There will be a slight bulge at this joint. You can work it out with your fingers kneading the carpeting back away from the chalk line. Be sure to match any pattern at this time.

6 Folding Back the Carpet. At the side walls, after the seam adhesive has dried, turn back the corners of the carpeting like a bedspread and fold the carpeting back.

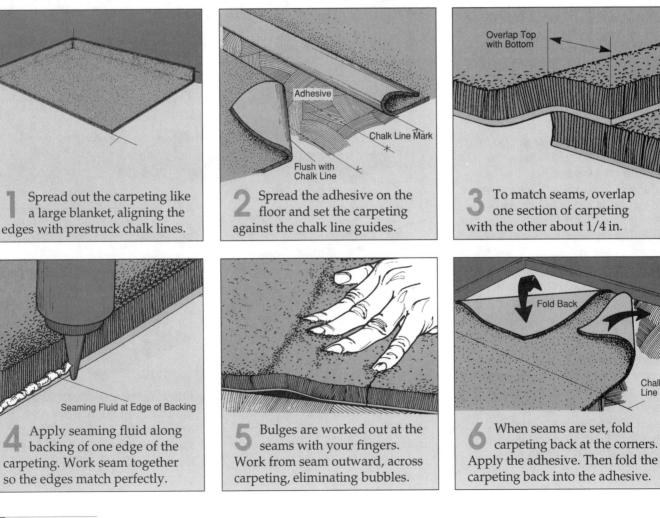

1 Spread out the carpeting like a large blanket, aligning the edges with prestruck chalk lines.

2 Spread the adhesive on the floor and set the carpeting against the chalk line guides.

3 To match seams, overlap one section of carpeting with the other about 1/4 in.

4 Apply seaming fluid along backing of one edge of the carpeting. Work seam together so the edges match perfectly.

5 Bulges are worked out at the seams with your fingers. Work from seam outward, across carpeting, eliminating bubbles.

6 When seams are set, fold carpeting back at the corners. Apply the adhesive. Then fold the carpeting back into the adhesive.

7 Applying the Adhesive. Use a notched trowel to apply the adhesive smoothly and evenly. Roll the folded carpeting back into the adhesive, working out any air bubbles as you go. If you notice an air bubble when the carpeting is installed, you can punch the backing with a sharp nail to release this air. However, try to work the carpeting into the adhesive so there is no air underneath the carpeting. Take your time and work slowly.

8 Trimming Excess Carpeting. Once the carpeting is down, you can install binder bars at doorways and set the carpeting to them, and trim excess carpeting away from the walls with a utility knife. Finally, go over the carpeting with a hammer and wooden buffer block, such as a short length of 2x4. Tap the face of the carpeting so it is firmed into the adhesive.

Chalk Line

7 Use a notched spreader to apply adhesive to the floor.

8 Trim carpeting with utility knife. Go over carpeting with hammer and wooden block.

Double-Faced Tape

The double-faced tape technique is not recommended for seaming foam-back carpet or carpets that receive a lot of foot traffic. If you use this method to install carpeting, unroll the carpeting and fit it to the measurements in the room. Place the tape around the edges of the room, sticking one side of the tape to the floor around the edges, and leaving the protective strip on the top of the tape. Position carpet over the tape. Then remove the protective strip in short lengths, and press carpeting to the tape. Once the carpeting is in place, you can trim the edges, if needed, with a utility knife.

Carpet Tile

Carpet tile is easy to use, even for the beginner. It can be installed by any one of three methods. The first calls for double-faced tape, while the second method uses carpet adhesives. The third takes advantage of a self-sticking back.

Carpet tiles are laid in the same way as resilient tile is laid, follow directions found on pages 47-52.

Using Double-Faced Tape. Place a square of tape in each corner of the individual tiles and press the tiles into place one by one.

Using Carpet Adhesive. This provides a more secure surface than the taping method. Use a trowel to spread adhesive over the floor. Follow the manufacturer's instructions carefully. Position the tiles exactly, and press them down firmly. Do not slide them around on the adhesive or up against each other.

Applying Self-Stick Tiles. This installation method utilizes self-sticking, foam-backed tiles. Peel the protective paper from the back of the tile, and position the tile in place. Firmly press the entire surface of the tile with the heel of your hand to seat the tiles securely. Align the tile exactly before placing it.

Finishing Carpet Edges

Begin finishing the carpet by creasing the edge with a stair tool or blunt-edged brick chisel. Create an edge in the carpeting with this tool (left). Once the edge has been formed, use a utility knife with a very sharp blade to trim away the carpeting. Take your time so the cut edge will be even and fit perfectly (middle). Now, with the tool or a rigid-bladed putty knife, firm the carpeting down onto the floor so the pile is wedged against the baseboard. The edge should look smooth and even (right).

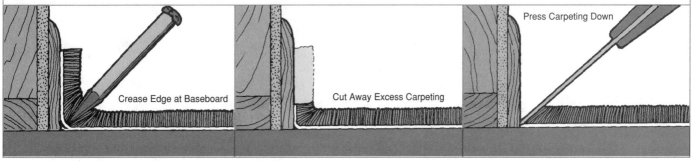

Crease Edge at Baseboard

Cut Away Excess Carpeting

Press Carpeting Down

Repairing Carpets

To make carpet repairs, you will need to have extra scraps of carpet from the original installation. The key to a successful carpet repair is to work patiently.

If there are no carpet scraps available, take patches for holes from unseen areas like the back of closets or under furniture you never move. Small areas often can be repaired by setting in new tufts with a tuftsetter, a machine that is available at most carpet dealers.

To patch a rip that has not damaged the backing, fold back the torn section and apply latex seam adhesive. Tuck the torn part back into the carpet and press it with a smooth rolling action using a large bottle. If adhesive oozes up, clean it with water and detergent. When the adhesive has dried, replace any loose or missing pile as explained below.

If the rip goes through the backing, release the tension, using a knee-kicker in the corner nearest the rip. Lift the corner off the tacks and roll it back. With thread to match the color of the pile, mend the rip with 1-inch-long stitches spaced 1/4 inch apart. Depending on the direction of the rip, run the stitches either parallel to rows of pile or perpendicular to them. Check frequently to make sure

Cut the damaged pile down to the backing with cuticle scissors. Pick out pile stubs with tweezers. Apply a little latex cement to the backing. Set replacement tufts, cut from the edge of a piece of scrap carpet, into the cement. For loop pile, poke one end of a long piece of yarn into backing and make successive loops, adjusting the length accordingly.

you are not stitching the pile down on the face of the carpet. Then work in a thin, wavy strip of adhesive and cover the wet backing with a paper towel. Roll the carpet back to the wall and rehook it on the tacks.

Always be aware of the carpet pattern and keep patches and tufts of pile tilted in the same direction as the rest of the carpet.

Patching a Large Area

1 Reducing Carpet Tension. Reduce the tension slightly with a knee-kicker, and tack down strips of carpet on all four sides of the damaged area.

2 Removing the Damaged Section. Use a screwdriver and framing square to gently separate carpet-pile tufts, exposing carpet backing along a square-cornered outline. Then, as shown, use a utility knife and framing square to cut through the carpet backing. Remove the damaged section. If the under-cushion is also damaged, cut and remove it, too. Repeating the same techniques, mark and cut a replacement patch the exact size of the removed section. (If the carpet has a pattern, first match the replacement section's pattern to it.)

3 Installing the Replacement Patch. Apply seam cement to the backing after slipping double-faced carpet tape partway under the existing carpet. Press the replacement patch carefully into place. To hide the seam, use the screwdriver to gently interweave pile tufts of the two pieces of carpeting.

1 To isolate the damage, use a knee-kicker to slacken tension as you tack upside-down strips of scrap carpet on all four sides.

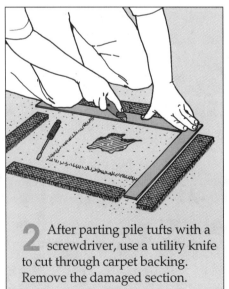

2 After parting pile tufts with a screwdriver, use a utility knife to cut through carpet backing. Remove the damaged section.

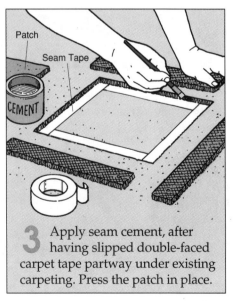

3 Apply seam cement, after having slipped double-faced carpet tape partway under existing carpeting. Press the patch in place.

Baseboard A piece of trim, either plain or milled, installed around a room at the base of the walls to conceal the joints of walls and adjoining floor covering.

Baseboard shoe A narrow piece of trim, usually quarter round, attached to the baseboard at the floor to hide any gaps.

Beam A horizontal structural member that sits on posts to support the floor joists.

Bedding block A block of wood that is covered with carpet or other protective strips and used to seat tiles in adhesive.

Blind nail Installation procedure for tongue-and-groove wood in which the nails are driven at an angle through the tongue and back into the body of the tile and the floor.

Building paper Also called felt paper or tar paper, used as a cushion or a moisture barrier between layers in a house, such as between a hardwood floor and the subfloor.

Carpet stretcher A device that grips the carpet and stretches it either with a force applied by the knee (to a knee-kicker, a small carpet stretcher) or mechanical force (in a larger power stretcher).

Caulking A soft compound for sealing joints against leaks (of water, air, or noise). It may be silicone, neoprene, acrylic, polyurethane, or one of a variety of other synthetic compounds.

Ceramic tile Fired clay tile that is hard and may be glazed or unglazed, 1 square inch or smaller to 1 square foot or larger in size, available in a profusion of colors, shapes, patterns, and textures.

Clear finish Any of a number of wood finishes that allow the wood grain to be seen.

Concrete A mixture of sand or gravel, Portland cement, and water that sets hard. Usually reinforced with wire mesh when poured for basement floors.

Control joints A shallow groove installed in a concrete slab to contain cracking within a given area.

Crawl space A low space above or below the house, just tall enough to permit such work as jacking up a sagging ground floor from below or installing ceiling fixtures above.

Cross bridging Diagonal braces between joists that keep them from bending out of line. Single diagonal braces are called bridging; they may be wood or metal.

Darby A flat, wide board with a handle used for the first smoothing of concrete just after it has been poured. These can be rented.

Finish flooring Any material such as parquet, tongue-and-groove planks, or continuous floor covering that is laid over subflooring. The exposed flooring.

Floorboard A board in a wood floor. Floorboards may be milled or not and are various lengths and widths.

Footing The concrete or masonry base supporting foundations, chimneys, and such structural members as posts.

Glazier's points Small wedges of metal most commonly used to hold a pane of glass in a window frame; also inserted between floorboards to silence squeaks.

Girder A main beam, usually running the length of a structure, that supports the floor joists and is itself supported by a post (or posts) in mid-span and at either end by the foundation.

Hardboard Sheet material composed of wood fibers compressed at high heat. The resulting material is quite hard.

In-fill Extra earth added beneath a concrete base to compensate for the falling off of the ground surface or to create a desired drainage pitch.

Joist A horizontal structural member that supports a floor and a ceiling, in the case of middle floors, and a ceiling alone in the case of a top floor. Joists are often tied together with cross bridging for extra rigidity.

Laminated wood tiles Built of layers of wood; especially appropriate for damp areas.

On center A phrase designating the distance between the centers of regularly spaced framing members, such as joists.

Open time The amount of time adhesive can stay on a floor before it dries out and no longer forms an effective bond.

Parquet A wood flooring material made into blocks or tiles; a finish wood flooring in a decorative design.

Reducing strip A trim tile used to finish an edge of a tile installation so the new and old floor levels meet in a smooth joint.

Row running cutter A knife for cutting carpeting that follows the rows of pile.

Saddle The strip under a door that joins the floors of two rooms by concealing the seam between them.

Screed Long piece of lumber (usually 2x4) drawn across concrete forms after a pour and used to strike off excess concrete, leveling a slab.

Sleepers Boards laid over a concrete floor as a foundation for the subflooring of a new floor.

Stain Any of various forms of water- or oil-based coloring agents, transparent or opaque, designed to penetrate the surface of wood.

Subfloor The floor surface below a finished floor. Usually made of sheet material like plywood; in older houses it is likely to consist of diagonal boards.

Sump A hole dug in the lowest corner of a basement to collect water from the floor so that it can be pumped away.

Tack cloth A piece of cheese cloth or other lint-free cloth treated with turpentine and a small amount of varnish to produce a tacky surface that picks up and holds dust and lint.

Tackless strip A thin strip of wood or metal in which many small, sharp teeth are imbedded to grip the edges of a wall-to-wall carpet when they are hooked over the teeth. The strip is nailed down; it takes its name from the amount of tacking it eliminates from carpet installation.

Tongue-and-groove The milling treatment of the edges of a board resulting in a protruding tongue on one side and groove the same size on the other. For the purpose of joining several boards.

Underlayment A smooth surface laid down to receive another surface, such as sheets of plywood under a ceramic-tile floor.

Vapor barrier Plastic sheeting used as a waterproof barrier to keep moisture in a concrete slab from penetrating finish flooring placed over it.

Weighted cloth A polishing cloth that is applied to the end of a mop handle or other device designed to add pressure during buffing.